FRESH INK

Essays from
Boston College's
First-Year Writing
Seminar, 1998

Edited by
Eileen Donovan-Kranz &
Lad Tobin

The McGraw-Hill Companies, Inc.
Primis Custom Publishing

New York St Louis San Francisco Auckland Bogotá
Caracas Lisbon London Madrid Mexico Milan Montreal
New Delhi Paris San Juan Singapore Sydney Tokyo Toronto

McGraw·Hill

A Division of The McGraw·Hill Companies

FRESH INK
Essays from Boston College's First-Year Writing Seminar, 1998

McGraw-Hill's Primis Custom Publishing consists of products that are
produced from camera-ready copy. Peer review, class testing, and accuracy
are primarily the responsibility of the author(s).

The opinions or views expressed in this work are those of the individual
authors (of the essays) and do not necessarily reflect the opinions or
recommendations of the editors of this work or Boston College.

1 2 3 4 5 6 7 8 9 0   BKM BKM   9 0 9 8

ISBN 0-07-229131-1

Editor: Debra Quigley
Manuscript Design and Preparation: Jakarta M. Eckhart, NiteOwl Creations
Cover Design: Jenny Jensen Greenleaf
Printer/Binder: Book-Mart Press, Inc.

Acknowledgments

$\mathcal{E}$ach spring amnesia strikes my co-editor, Lad Tobin, and me as we begin to piece this book — *Fresh Ink* — together. But it's a convenient affliction that allows us, as we sit down to read many hundred student essay submissions, to forget just how much work it is to complete this project. We always seem to think that the current stage of the project is the toughest, and the last, and we forget the myriad steps that lie ahead. This was true even this year, with the production of this, the fifth (as always, all new!) edition of *Fresh Ink: Essays from Boston College's First-Year Writing Seminar.*

Strangely, even though that amnesiac fog descends annually, there is one thing we never forget: the people we can count on to help us bring this book to fruition. For all those people listed below, the depth of our gratitude is great.

First and foremost we thank all those student writers who submitted essays in December and May. Each year that we read the hundreds of submissions is like an immersion course in so many things: the pulse of a time; the weight of a human heart; the interests, passions, aggravations, obsessions, fascinations. . .curiosities of one writer after another, and another. We thank each essayist for submitting work for consideration for this project. We particularly thank the twenty-five essayists selected here for allowing us to publish their fine essays. The First-Year Writing Seminar benefits immeasurably from this collection of student writing.

Our reading committee we thank for the long hours of reading, pondering and arguing spent in the Carney Conference Room during some hot days in May. Those readers include: Beth Dacey, Andrea Defusco, John Dunn, Mark Dursin, Annie Lugthart, Jillian Pagliocca and Susan Roberts.

We appreciate all seventy of our FWS instructors for their care with students and their expertise in the field. The following teachers worked with the student writers herein: Treseanne Ainsworth, Amelia Audette, Beth Dacey, Andrea Defusco, Eileen Donovan-Kranz, John Dunn, Dayton Haskin, Diane Hotten-Somers, Melissa Kenney, James Leonard, Paul Lewis, Annie

Lugthart, Marybeth McLean, Tyler McDaniel, Joseph O'Malley, Karen Paley and Susan Roberts.

English Department members Claudette Picklesimer, Judy Plank, Patrice Scott and all our work-study students we thank for their time, support and patience with nitty gritty production details. Lucy Tobin we thank, as always, for her interest and savvy advice.

For the lovely look of this year's cover, we thank graphic designer Jenny Jensen Greenleaf; for the judicious and talented copy editing we send our appreciation to Alan Huisman. Thanks also to Debbie Quigley and Don Golini of McGraw-Hill Custom Publishers.

Finally, every good writer hopes that a final product reads effortlessly and well, with no evidence of the hair-pulling aggravation it may have intermittently caused its author. Editors of essay collections hope so, too. Despite the hurdles of a lengthy production process (we begin planning for the next book once this edition hits the bookstore), this is a beloved project. Therefore, we thank *you* for reading this book.

—EDK

Table of Contents

Alternate Arrangement of Essays

Essays Organized Alphabetically

Introduction

*O*nce I had an English teacher for whom I could do nothing right. I tried hard to jazz up each paper but I suppose my attempts at adornment were a problem — like gluing buckles and bows to ill-fitting shoes. Deep down I knew the real problem and, honestly, I was surprised a teacher (of all people) could diagnose it too: I wasn't interested in the assignments.

But then a strange thing happened, something from either a fairytale or the conclusion of a teenage sitcom. My teacher read an article I wrote for the student newspaper, a comic send-up of teenage disco culture (I'm dating myself, now) — and then, she *apologized* to me. In that article she could see, she said, that I really was a very good writer.

Today that apology strikes me as more strange than magical — one good article hardly undid the mediocrity of those earlier essays — but at the time I felt as any teenager would: smug and victorious. For I finally had turned my teacher into my reader (maybe this *is* a fairy tale), and that reader felt the way I did while writing: interested.

It's fair to say that this personal story is not so personal, for the theme here is transformation and in FWS that is what we hope — no, indeed, *work* — for. Over the weeks, teachers become readers, students, writers. Certainly, as teachers, we are more interested when our students are engaged by material of their own choosing, material of deep interest, whether that interest derives from intellectual curiosity, comedic impulse, moral outrage, personal annoyance, political insight, abiding memory. We hear from our students, and we know from their writing, that students prefer to work this way, too.

In this book you'll find essays of many shapes and kinds. And we had so many essays to chose from: over four hundred submissions this year. (Another emblem of our students' engagement with the course, the subject matter, their own work.) Each essay we chose is surely *interesting*: for the story, for the meaning, for the voice, for the thinking, for the message. A casual reader of this book may alternately be entertained, moved, informed, maddened or persuaded by the essays within. Maybe inspired.

We hope so. A careful reader of this collection might even infer the themes and methods of our course from these products. At the most elemental, we encourage student writers to come up with ideas, then to challenge and test and stretch them, to try new forms of writing, to revise again and again, to match idea to method to intended audience. And of course, to read. As evident from the selections here, writers in this course produce essays across a broad spectrum. Over the course of a semester, they must. In this way, students of FWS find their voices, develop as thinkers and writers, test and reject assumptions, find literary and intellectual idols and nemeses, polish their prose and prepare for the world.

And though you can't tell from the finished products, each of these pieces is in some way about transformation — from rough idea to polished product, from hazy question to researched inquiry, from memory to meaningful narrative, from observation to journalistic authority.

And finally, from students to authors.

Eileen Donovan-Kranz
Assistant Director of Writing
Summer 1998

Part One

Narrative

Kickball Champion of the World

Chris Tarantino

Kickball was life.

Even though, like all eight-year-old girls, I played Barbies with careless abandon, had sparkle shoelaces for my sneakers, and really didn't care too much about sports one way or the other, I was hopelessly drawn to that universal recess obsession. I longed to feel the rush of a perfectly executed kick, the exhilaration of running that victory lap around the bases. Of course, our games were much too short to allow time for victory laps in the first place . . . but it was the principle: the awestruck looks from fellow classmates as the winning team went straight to the head of the recess line (even if every single person's last name began with T), the way someone would always volunteer to feed the class gerbil for you on the days you scored a home run. Kickball victories demanded a certain respect, and I, like everyone else, craved that recognition.

Unfortunately, one thing stood in my way.

Make that one *person.* Known throughout the school as Kickball Champion of the World, Neil was Moses parting the Red Sea when he stepped into a crowd of us. Towering, brutelike fourth-grade boys would step aside in the halls to let him pass. Rumor had it Neil was actually eleven years old and had stayed back, year after year, just so he would never lose his title. It was a believable theory. We all knew he was destined for the Olympics, and experts gave him roughly two more years of third grade before he was scouted for the pros. Both admired and feared, he was a living icon of third-grade lore; something superhuman and beyond our comprehension.

He never had to feed the gerbil.

I'm not sure when I decided Neil had held his title for too long or what possessed me to think I could take it away from him. I knew I was messing with the gods . . . but I felt somehow guided by a higher force, a desire to overcome this obstacle that stood in the way of every third grader's dream. Granted, I was afraid. Legend had it that during Neil's second year of third grade someone had attempted to dethrone him with the complex and mysterious Four-Fingered Pitch. Neil kicked that ball so hard and so far, it landed in the yard of the house next door. The pitcher was understandably shattered by the incident and for the rest of the year developed sudden recurring headaches that kept him in the nurse's office during recess instead of out on the kickball field. After a couple of years, nobody saw him again. The story goes that he moved to Fort Worth with his parents. . . but some of us believe he just disappeared. Trauma does that sort of thing to a person.

Olympic talent aside, Neil ruled us by our fear. I'd heard all the stories, and a part of me knew that what I was trying to do was potentially very dangerous and could permanently break my psyche. Therefore, I kept my plans to myself, not even confiding in my best friend. Who was to say she wouldn't think me as foolhardy as that boy from years ago? Nevertheless, It was time he learned what it felt like to stand at the back of the line, to feed the gerbil.

This was my mission.

Every night for almost a week I practiced in my backyard, undertaking rigorous training regimens until Brendan's mother would come over from next door and ask me to please stop kicking things against the fence because it made the dog jumpy.

Tired and sore, I entered school on Thursday determined and confident. I could feel the puzzled looks of my classmates, their whispered questions as I stalked onto the field at recess. Neil stood apart, unaffected by my presence. I waited at home plate, my heart racing, as he twisted the rubber ball around and around in his hand, looking nonchalantly into the sky as if waiting for some divine signal to begin the game.

And then he saw me.

Across the asphalt our eyes locked and for a moment my heart stopped completely. The playground seemed to go silent, and the space between us telescoped until I felt I could reach out and grab the ball away. A muscle in Neil's face twitched as we stared each other down. I could almost hear his brain working, deciding which particular pitch would utterly crush me. I thought fleetingly of the people who had crossed Neil . . . about their fate. I wondered what the rest of the school year would be like observed from the inside of the nurse's office. I felt sweat break out on my forehead. I was petrified.

But somehow I didn't look away.

In slow motion I watched the corners of his mouth curl up in a sneer. He'd seen third graders come and go for ages; he could handle me. His arm swung back so far that the ball was momentarily lost from view. My face felt frozen; my arms hung limply at my sides. Neil's muscles tensed beneath his Voltron T-shirt . . . and suddenly the ball was coming toward me at an impossible speed. In the back of my mind I remembered the Four-Fingered Pitch as my foot connected with the textured rubber.

Time stopped.

The ball was *soaring*. Every face on the playground turned upward, watching the perfect arc of the ball as it went higher and higher and farther and farther. My own jaw dropped. I didn't remember how to run, where to put my feet.
"Home run!" somebody shouted, and I knew I needed to move. It still depended on me.
But it was Neil who was running.
With arms outstretched he ran back and back, face tilted toward the sky. There was a panic about him I had never seen before, and I started running too, determined to reach my goal. Neil was momentarily lost to my vision as I ran and ran and ran . . . closer to first base . . . nearer to the triumph that would salvage this moment.

"Out!"

I heard the thump of the ball against his chest before the word registered in my mind. It seemed to echo as my sneaker slammed against the chalked-in base. As if underwater, I slowly turned my head. Neil sat on the pavement, the ball in his lap, a look of undisguised wonder overflowing his face. And then I fell, shocked, to the ground as well.

Later, in line, I stood in the back with all the rest of the people with last names beginning with T and I sulked. I hadn't even been given the chance to make it to base. There was nothing I could do about Neil. He would be in third grade forever, eternally haunting recess, making it impossible to enjoy the game. I had tried to change all that, and I had failed. It was the fate of anyone who crossed him. I was no different.

"Hey."

It was Neil, of course. This insult added to injury was almost too much to bear. I cringed in anticipation of whatever hurtful thing he felt he needed to say to me.

"You play pretty well, you know," he grunted in that way he had," for a girl."

That was it. He left and went to the front of the line where the rest of his teammates were waiting. I felt strange. Although the embarrassment of my failure still stung, I couldn't help but feel I had just been witness to something legendary. Neil the Great . . . the Kickball Champion of the World . . . had complimented me. He had recognized my effort and the potential talent that lay somewhere underneath. I stood straighter, looking at the back of his head past the line of students in front of me. I felt almost proud of him, my frustration dissolving as it occurred to me that he *was* perhaps the greatest kickball player I knew.

But I still didn't volunteer to feed the gerbil.

The Committee

Mary E. Sullivan

Route 1 rose and quickly fell away again as my father pushed his foot down on the accelerator. He had been driving since he was twelve, and after forty-four years he had not yet lost his love for speed. I glanced into the back seat, which was teeming with packages and bags from our early-morning shopping. The two of us had settled into a pattern, getting up early Saturday mornings and finishing the weekend errands as soon as possible. It gave us the rest of the weekend to relax, but more often than not we ended up doing "homework" as soon as we returned to the house. His, of course, was from the office, but I teased him about it nonetheless.

The clock on the dashboard read 11:45 A.M., and we decided to stop on the way home for a bite to eat. We always ended up at IHOP, but we went through the motions of considering the merits of nine or ten different restaurants on the way. As we pulled into the driveway of the restaurant, Dad made a wisecrack about being able to park in the handicapped space because of my mental condition, and I playfully retorted that his huge nose would never be able to fit into such a small area. Our relationship, while sincerely loving and sensitive, had always been oiled by our ability to tease one another. On these mornings we felt more like friends than father and daughter.

I opened the door and stepped out into the warm summer air, stretching for a moment and lifting my face to the sunshine. Turning quickly, I grabbed my purse and slammed the door shut, and then noticed that my father was staring at me, his eyes burning with an illuminating intensity that I knew only too well.

"Are you okay, Dad?" The question was only a formality. I knew the answer before it left his mouth. "Yes, I'm fine. It's just that you remind me so much of your mother."

The kitchen table was overflowing with goodies, and the aromas floating in the air around my nose were assurances of a heavenly feast in the making. I had never seen so much food before except for holidays and funerals and weddings. I thought it must be a very important meeting for so many of my mom's friends to get together and cook so much. When I asked my mother why everyone was acting as if the weekend reunion was such a big deal, she just smiled.

"It is a big deal, honey. All of my best friends are together again."

I didn't understand what my mother meant, so I shrugged and returned to the basement to play Barbie with my sister and all the other children. As I placed my foot on the last step, I heard a burst of laughter and a jumble of jokes and shrieks and giggles. Why were they being so silly? This was not how a mom was supposed to act, and yet it happened every time she got together with the Committee.

Committee meetings were so few and far between that they ranked just behind church and just ahead of a weekend alone with my father. The Committee was a special, elite coalition. It consisted of my mother and her five best friends, all of whom had met in kindergarten and hadn't parted company since. Membership lasted a lifetime. The meetings changed location and and were held at intervals of weeks or years. The only defining mark of the Committee schedule was that they would always meet again.

And so they did. The final one was at Mom's best best friend's house, in Wisconsin, which was only about four hours away from our small town in Minnesota. The house, especially the kitchen, was engulfed in a haze of merriment. Laughter was never-ending as my mother and her friends sipped their wine and took drags from one another's cigarettes (although none of them smoked on a regular basis).

"Do you need some more coffee, there's enough for—"

" I heard she was dating a client of—"

"Have you seen my husband? He's not in the living room."

They talked and chatted and laughed in an encrypted dialect that only they could decipher, and the years came and went as memories of friends and family were recounted. The rest of the world went on without them as they laughed together, as only true friends can do.

My father paid the bill while I went outside to unlock the car, and I thought about what he had said. I reminded him so much of Mom. But who was she? What kind of person was she really? What were her interests? These were questions I had asked myself thousands of times in the eight years since she had died. I was struggling to find out who my mother was so that I could also find out who I had the potential to become.

As my dad eased himself into the driver's seat, he glanced at me again, and I could see the light shining in his eyes. We often spoke about

Mom during our Saturday mornings together. He loved to talk about her. It was one of his favorite things to do, yet he never seemed overbearing about it or incapable of leaving the past behind. He had told me about the first time they met, their honeymoon in Lake Tahoe, and the first years of their marriage. I had compiled all this information in my mind, interweaving it with my own memories of my mother: the night she had let me stay up to see an Elvis special on the Disney Channel, our first New Year's celebration, when I was eight and allowed to join in. These memories and many more had been accumulating and taking shape in my mind, forming a picture by which I could identify my mom.

"She loved you very much, you know. You were our little girl, our miracle baby. She loved you and she would have done anything for you."

I know, Dad. I had learned through my father the kind of love and support that is necessary for a family to survive. But the memories of my mom and her Committee had given me an idea of what friendships were like.

The next meeting of the Committee was three years later, at my mother's funeral. They sat together in a huddled group, as if to support one another. There were no words spoken between them. I watched them throughout the entire Mass— I couldn't tear my eyes away from their shuddering bodies. As they wept, I felt ashamed for not being able to cry. The only thing I felt was a dull ache and a hollow pain in the pit of my stomach. I envied them for being able to let go, to mourn and not consider the consequences of their public display. I did not have the courage or the audacity to break down as they did. I didn't have that luxury.

As the priest performed the final rights over my mother's casket, I glanced over at Mom's friend Penny. She looked up and tried to smile, to put on a brave face. It was then I noticed the space between her body and the rest of the Committee members. There remained a gap just large enough for a small child. It puzzled me; instead of turning my attention to the front, I kept my gaze on the pew. Soon I could see my mother's outline. Her tiny frame, her delicate face and elegant stature, came into focus in my mind's eye. She was looking at me, her mouth smiling, her brilliant blue eyes shining. There was a light surrounding her, and then she was gone. I looked once again at Penny's face, at the tears and sorrow and pain, and I laughed. I laughed because my mother had been with her sisters one last time. And then I cried.

There is a light in Dad's eyes when he speaks of my mother. A sparkle that appears in his eyes, and in the Committee members', whenever her name is mentioned. It is her spirit. I have spent so many hours with the Committee and my father, sharing and reliving the miracle of my

mother's life. She was a caring and loving woman, and it was her selflessness and devotion to the Committee girls that had made their friendships
last. There is no scientific formula for finding love of any kind and certainly none for keeping it. Those six women—Penny, Sheila, Gretchen, Anne,
Barbara, and my mother, Susan—attained and maintained what can truly
be described as an eternal friendship. Its secret lies in the selflessness of the
members. I can only hope that one day I will be a part of a love like that.

Terrace

Bruno de Faria

❦

The school van slowly made its way through the dense São Paulo traffic. My privileged front seat allowed me to gaze at the familiar city sights. On the corner of First and Thirtieth a happy couple walked hand in hand, helping their toddler make his way to the local park. Down the street music rang from a local hangout; people filled its outdoor terrace, talking and playing cards. The sun seemed reluctant to set, and the purple haze it made when joined with the city's heavy smog was surprisingly beautiful. The van found a bit of freedom in the decongesting traffic. The breeze made its way through the window and I put my arm out to feel the cool wind. The driver smiled and warned me about getting my arm caught by a speeding mail carrier or pizza delivery boy riding on motorbikes; they swerved between cars like slalom skiers. I told him I'd be careful. He was a nice man, around thirty, with a wife and a small daughter. I'd see him around the neighborhood and always on Sundays at church. My stop was coming up so I quietly woke my little brother. He was eight years old, I ten. I always thought of the two years separating us as minimal, but he was still young enough to sleep on the way home.

The driver stopped the van. I said good-bye and headed toward the main door of the apartment building. It was a modern thirteen-story high-rise typical of large cities. The guard recognized my brother and me and let us in. We entered the wide, ample lounge containing numerous elevators. We took the appropriate elevator and headed up to the eleventh floor, where our mom was waiting with the door open. She kissed us both and directed us toward the kitchen. It was my favorite time of the day. The kitchen always seemed to smell better in the afternoon. The almost dying sun warmed the tiles, and the smell of freshly baked cake was very inviting. Happily leaving the worries of school at the door, my brother and I lounged in the kitchen and then watched TV with our mom before my dad got home from work. The afternoon wound down, and I went out on the terrace. The terrace was my favorite place in the apartment. I could be both inside and out, be involved in the everyday activities of the household and at the same time be an observer.

From the eleventh floor everything looked different. It was as if a lens had been placed on the world. The view was incredible, the silhouettes of the apartment buildings against the darkness of the night and the splendor of the lights. The full moon reflecting on the river evoked the tranquillity of a small country town within this huge cosmopolitan city. The music from the local bars filtered up even to the eleventh floor. Inside I could hear my dad talking to my brother about a soccer game or something.

I sat and studied all that lay before me. Across from our apartment building was another, about fifteen yards away. I could see what was going on inside every household. I knew it was wrong, but I couldn't help looking; half the time it wasn't even intentional. One story down, a father and mother were having what appeared to me to be a serious conversation. Occasionally a teenage girl, about sixteen, would appear in the living room where the two were talking. That was where the biggest window was. It was like the one at my house, a large glass sliding door. To the left of the terrace was the room of the remaining member of the household. A young man, around twenty, lay on his bed staring up at the ceiling. The only light came from a small table lamp on his desk in the far corner. It was kind of dark in that room, so it was hard to see. The girl's room was to the right of the living/dining room. She went into her room and made a telephone call. The parents remained in the living room, sipping wine and talking calmly. It was like watching a movie, or several movies showing on several televisions in the same room.

Inside my dad was preparing the VCR and my mom was making popcorn for the weekly Friday-night family movie. I stayed on the terrace a while longer, looking up at the stars. They seemed so far off, so distant. All I could hear was the occasional blare of a horn from the traffic below. It was strange how a city so large could seem so peaceful, so empty. It was getting late, I needed to go inside, but I glanced over again at the family in front. The girl seemed to be having a grand time. She was still talking on the phone, laughing and talking. Talking to a friend, probably, about trivial, everyday things. What time they would meet at the mall tomorrow morning, whether the boy sitting behind them at lunch today was cute or not, how hard their homework was, the problems they had with their parents. . . . She was in her own world. My attention was drawn to the young man.

He had gotten up and was now sitting on the edge of the bed with his face in his hands. It was evident that he was crying. At my young age it was strange to see an adult, or at least a young adult, crying. He got up from the bed, stared into the mirror hanging on the back of the door. He dried his eyes, turned around and sat in the chair in the corner. There was a piece of paper on the desk. He opened the drawer, took out a pen, and began writing something on the paper. Then my mom called me, the movie was about to start. I looked at the family one last time. The mom and dad weren't in the living room anymore; they'd moved on to the kitchen, the mom washing the dishes and the dad drying them. I imagined their conversation in my head. *We have to get him some help. It's our fault. No it's not; we've been there for him his whole life. What did we do, where did we go wrong?* I went inside.

The popcorn tasted good and the movie wasn't bad either. But just when the plot was beginning to unravel there was this loud noise outside, a sound one would hear at a construction site, a sound of heavy dropping or banging. We all jumped, and I rushed onto the terrace. On the ground, eleven stories down, lay the sprawled body of the young man from in front. He was next to a palm tree and looked normal except that his head was turned in a peculiar way. There was a puddle of blood forming at the base of his head. Slowly a small congregation formed around the body. They were getting a close-up view of something only seen in movies or the eleven o'clock news. No one attempted any emergency CPR; the young man was clearly dead. I stared from the safety of the eleventh floor. The family in front must have realized what had happened; the house was empty, a broken dish on the kitchen floor, a phone off the hook.

An ambulance siren sounded in the distance. The mom appeared on the scene a minute later. She ran to the body, breaking through the wall of bodies separating her from her son. She sank down next to him in an attempt to call him back, to convince him that it was worth living, to say sorry, to ask him why. She knelt beside him for what seemed like hours, crying, holding his bruised head on her lap. The father knelt beside her, and for the second time that day I saw a grown man cry. He stared up at the sky with a questioning look. Why had this fallen upon his family? The sister stood crying beside them, a bewildered look on her face. Soon the ambulance arrived and the crowd diminished. A paramedic placed the young man on a stretcher. The mother sat on the damp, cold concrete and watched her son being wheeled away. She sat and watched as he rolled through this, their, street for the last time. This street, where he had learned to ride a bike, learned to drive, had run naked as a child on hot, humid summer days, was now a symbol of his end. This street bore nothing of him except the bloodstain near the palm tree. And that stain would also, with time, fade away.

The parents went up to their empty home. I felt ashamed but couldn't help looking one last time at the house in front. The father entered his son's room and the last thing I saw from that terrace was the father closing his son's window. It took me a month before could I go out on the terrace again.

My parents knew what had happened. They asked me if I was okay and I answered that I was. My brother looked at me with fascination; I had seen a real dead body, wow. My dad let me sleep in my parent's bed that night. As I lay there in between my dad and my mom, I wondered what had driven that young man to kill himself. I lay there feeling sorry for a mother, for a father, and for a sister. And for a long time I lay there feeling scared.

I'll Never Forget Again

Brendan Caffrey

Running up the outside steps of the empty house, the boy, clad as always in his blue-and-yellow-plaid parochial school uniform, opens the old wooden door with its single lock. As he enters he shouts, "Grandma, I'm home!" As usual she responds, "Who's there?" An odd comment, as this ritual takes place every day. He plays the role as he has learned it. "It's me!"

He runs upstairs and enters the cold and lonely apartment, which is silent except for the low squeak of the hamster in his cage. He is alone, as always. It isn't all that bad. His parents will be home soon enough, and until then, if he needs anything there is Grandma downstairs. She will look after him. It's a comfort to the young boy. He loves being on his own, loves the independence. But he is only a boy. He still searches for Mommy every time he walks through that door, knowing full well she won't, can't be there. He is alone, on his own at eleven. But if he needs anything Grandma is there.

From the room where I was sleeping, I heard her cry out. Or maybe I didn't even hear her. Did I really have to? I knew she had fallen again. I ran from my bed as if hearing an alarm, flying to her aid. I picked her off the carpet and moved her aching body into the bed. This was the worst part, a moment of clarity. It was after she fell that she would have these moments. A brief period where the Alzheimer's that distorted her every thought and action would melt away. I was frightened, but not nearly as much as she was. She knew. She knew her mind was going. She knew how crazy she sounded. And even worse, she knew there was nothing she could do about it. She would cry. So there I was, with an eighty-four-year-old woman crying in my arms, apologizing for being such a burden, apologizing for keeping me awake, apologizing for doing all these crazy things. At four in the morning I had no response to make to her.

The boy makes plans on the phone to visit a friend. Before he leaves, all plans have to be cleared with Grandma. She never says no. "Grandma, I'm going up to Scott's," the boy shouts, hoping to escape without interrogation yet knowing full well he cannot. "Who's that!" Her response to everything. The boy realizes, as he always does, that he will have to go in and talk to her. He makes the routine responses to her questions: "Scott lives up the street, Grandma . . . yes, Mom knows him . . . yes, I'll be home for dinner . . . okay, I'll put a jacket on." He runs out with the large plastic bat in his hand, annoyed at losing quality whiffle ball time. Seeing an unusual number of people outside Scott's house the boy runs to investigate. Always with a big mouth, the brave yet scrawny eleven-year-old shouts some choice words at the unwelcome additions to the block, inviting them to kiss here and there. Then the fighting starts. The boy is small and his yellow T-shirt and blue jeans do not conceal this fact. After a few moments he is on the ground. No stranger to fights, he assumes the position his brothers have taught him, covering his face and ribs while trying in vain to roll himself into a ball. After an all-too-long while the aggressors grow tired of this activity and allow the scrappy eleven-year-old a chance to run. He does. Knowing the neighborhood as he does, he quickly loses his pursuers.

The day had finally come. They were moving my grandmother into a nursing home. My parents had finally decided the burden was too much for us. Even with a nurse on duty during the day and me sleeping down there every night, she needed more care. Her hallucinations had become more and more dangerous. She would get up at three in the morning and get ready to go to a job she hadn't held in over twenty years. I would have to battle with her to get her not to leave. She would fall, often. It was too much. Each fall hurt my mother more then it did my aging grandmother. My mother had tried to avoid this day. The nursing home was a death sentence, and the whole family knew it. The battle was over, and we had lost.

I breathed a silent sigh of relief. For me this meant no more sleepless nights. I no longer had to convince a crazy old lady that the man on the television wasn't talking to her. I no longer had to peel this woman, whom I once thought to be so strong, off her bedroom floor. Now she was someone else's burden, not mine. I wouldn't have to deal with any more moments of clarity that only I had the opportunity to witness. This was freedom. My mother wept; I couldn't console her. I felt no pain, no remorse, only freedom.

Guilt? I felt none. I was sixteen years old. I wasn't a nurse. I wasn't a trained professional. How dared they expect me to be! How dared they place this burden on me! I was never asked. And even if I had been, how could I say no? Why should I feel guilt? I'd given all I could. I was drained, emotionally, physically. I had nothing more to give her. I felt as if she had stolen my youth. But who could I blame? Who should I blame? Her, my grandmother?

The boy comes home, the mixture of tears and blood still fresh on his face. He is hurt, upset, and frightened by the experience, which one would think he would be used to by now. He is not. There is not a person alive who doesn't get scared. Despite his tough-guy bravado, this boy is no different. What scares this boy? The bullies? Hardly. No, this brazen big-mouth is more afraid of sitting in his house, alone and hurt, than anything else in the world.

His grandmother, hearing his tears, goes up to the empty apartment to be with him. She knows he has gotten into another fight. His mother will be upset if she finds out. She won't. This small escapade, like many others, is a secret. One shared by the boy and his grandmother. One that will never be spoken of. His grandmother will clean his wounds, comfort him, and yes, even scold him a little. But tell on him, never. When Mom comes home from work, this afternoon's saga will be a thing of the past. The boy knows it and loves his grandmother for it. But he loves her even more for just being there.

After about a year and half in the nursing home, my grandmother passed away. I had slept in her apartment every night for nearly three years. I felt bitter. I hated it, all of it. Trying to deal with an Alzheimer's patient was no way for a teenager to spend his evenings. At her wake the family priest asked me to share something that I learned from my grandmother. I had nothing to say. I couldn't share a pleasant memory, an adage, or an anecdote. All I could remember were the sleepless nights, the falls, and most of all the moments of clarity. I cried. I had forgotten our secrets. I had forgotten the comfort. I had forgotten the great woman that my grandmother once was. I had forgotten it all.

I never understood why my parents made me stay down there with her. They knew I hated it. I couldn't do anything for her that a nursing home couldn't have done better. Or so I thought. In retrospect, when my grandmother fell there isn't a place on this earth I would have rather been than at her side. To this day I haven't told my mother about the moments of clarity. Maybe because it would hurt her too much to know how my grandmother suffered. Or maybe because in some way I feel I owe it to my grandmother. I had forgotten everything, even our secrets. I'll never forget again.

Heroes' Journey

TML

After the Vietnam War ended in 1975, the communists took over South Vietnam and its capital, Saigon. Eventually my family was forced to leave the country. We had to leave our home, our relatives, and all our belongings and take a long boat journey to America. My three oldest brothers went first, joining my father and uncle, who were already there. My brothers left Vietnam two and half years before I did because if they had stayed, they would have been drafted to invade Cambodia as part of the same army that had murdered our neighbors and destroyed our lives.

Many South Vietnamese fled the country after the victory of Ho Chi Minh's army. Those who failed to escape paid with their lives. In the novel, *All the Pretty Horses*, Cormac McCarthy says, "It is supposed to be true that those who do not know history are condemned to repeat it." My mother doesn't believe that knowing can save her. The constants in history are greed and foolishness and love, and these are things that even God— who knows all that can be known—seems powerless to change. Since my mother wanted her children to have a better life, she was willing to try to escape.

It was a dark, cold, windy morning in 1982. I was four years old. My mother, three of my brothers, and I boarded a small fishing boat out of Vietnam. The gloomy atmosphere bespoke misfortune, but we knew that God was there to help us. Our dreams and hope would guide us safely to America. For five days, thirty-six people watched anxiously for a glimpse of the new land.

On the second day of our journey we ran into a ship. At first we were happy to see it. We thought it was a rescue ship. Sailors from the ship boarded our boat and gave us food, but then they took out their guns and threatened to kill us all if we did not give them our money and gold. There was no choice but to give them what we had. They searched our boat thor-

oughly for any hidden valuables and raped the few young girls. The screaming of these girls still echoes in my mother's head sometimes. It was a
nightmare, but there wasn't much the people on our boat could do about it.
Our fear had taken over our brains. One man tried to stop a pirate from
dragging his daughter away and got a bullet through his head. He fell into
the ocean, and his blood spread out into the cold, blue water. I will remember this image for life. It has left a scar, and the events that caused it can
never be forgotten, though the scar is mental and abstract, not physical and
concrete.

　　　That same day we ran into a severe storm that crippled the engine,
and our boat drifted aimlessly for two days. I was thirsty, and I asked my
mother for a drink. When she walked to the back of the boat where the
water containers were kept, she found several ignorant crew members
dumping the water into the ocean: if the boat was wrecked, they planned
to use the containers as life preservers. She did not blame them for what
they had done. When danger strikes us, we protect ourselves. There is good
and evil within all of us.

　　　God was watching us; without his help we would never have survived. He sent a fishing boat to save us. The people on the fishing boat
gave us food, fuel, and directions to head inland, to Thailand. When we got
there, a patrol boat fired at us, forcing us back toward the open sea. Even as
we signaled an SOS , machine-gun bullets ripped into the water, fifteen feet
from our boat. We retreated into international waters.

　　　The people on the boat had come a long way, and they were not
about to give up. Courage comes more easily in times of crisis. At night, we
returned; about a hundred feet from shore, we crowded into the one small
lifeboat and paddled inland. The next morning, United Nations officials
found us on the beach. We were saved.

　　　Finally we were in a new land, one that had no communists, but it
was not the land in which we wanted to be. The United Nations officials
processed us into a Thailand refugee camp, carefully leaving our accounts
of the gunboat assault out of our statements. The camp was an old prison
no longer in use; all the bars had been taken out. We were placed on the
second floor. There were no beds; everyone slept on the floor. The hard,
cold cement floor made many people sick, including my mother, but every
day she managed to get up and feed her children. This journey was not
easy for my mother, but throughout it she thought of her children's needs
first, even though many other parents abandoned their children in desperation. My brother told me she once ate only the skin of an apple, giving
me all the flesh.

Our days in the camp were very long and tiresome. There wasn't much to do. All we had was our hope and our dream that our family would be reunited. For two long years, we stayed in the refugee camp, until that morning in 1984 when we were admitted to the United States. Our family was united again, but our arrival in America was not the end of our struggle. There were further obstacles to overcome in order to "normalize" our lives. But can our lives ever be normal?

In their journey to find a better a life, some people pay a big price, in blood. Fortunately, we were not asked to pay with our lives. But our near-death experiences have made us realize and value life more than ever before. Freedom fighters, with their courage, strength, and determination, are the heroes of this world. In our search for freedom our family had to leave our homeland. We left all our belongings and our relatives and traveled halfway around the world. We would have paid with our lives if we had not succeeded. We were fortunate that we did succeed, but nothing comes easy. The price of any hero's journey is tremendously high.

Through the Kitchen Door

Pauline Mulleady

There it was again, that all-too-familiar feeling in the pit of my stomach every time I walked down the aisle toward the teacher's desk to receive yet another reprimand. I had come to the United States only a short time ago, and already I could tell you exactly the number of black linoleum floor tiles between my desk and Mrs. Gorrin's.

I had absolutely no clue what I would be admonished about this time, but since I was practically failing school at the ripe old age of eight, I was ready for just about anything. It turned out that the problem was no fault of mine but arose from Mrs. Gorrin's lack of cultural awareness— although she didn't quite see it that way. She was having trouble understanding how I could put a check mark next to every single problem on the paper I had graded and still manage to give it a grade of 100%. I explained that in Ireland a check mark designated a correct answer and an X represented a wrong one. Looking rather confused and disbelieving, she ushered me back to my desk. Then, using words that would haunt me for years—"That's not how things are done around here"— she told me to get rid of all of my check marks. As if this weren't bad enough, she went on to give me a week's detention when I quite innocently asked her for a big green rubber to aid me in my task. It wasn't until years later in health class that l learned that a "rubber" in this country had a slightly different definition than the one of "eraser" in Ireland.

Needless to say, I was having trouble making the transition to the American life-style. I had given up trying to learn American spellings. I was spending recess in speech therapy (which I thought odd, since English is spoken in Ireland). Mrs. Gorrin's approach to mathematics was contrary to anything I had ever learned, and I was flunking that subject miserably. However, none of it phased me in the least. I felt fate, the master of my destiny, had dealt me a terrible wrong by wrenching me out of Ireland, and as a result it was sure to cut me a little slack to make up for it. (How much slack is another issue, but like any other upstanding preadolescent, I was willing to test my boundaries and find out.) At that age the whole world is basically confined to the block we live on, and our parents are the most powerful beings on it. Fate and my father and mother were one and the same, forming a sort of Holy Trinity, which meant, as far as I was concerned, that it was their fault we had to leave Ireland. I certainly was never consulted; no one threw the idea in my direction. So my refusals to blend into my new environment and try to adjust were my first true rebellion.

Precisely how long I would have ventured down this road of self-destruction is unsure, but I might still be on it if it weren't for one life-changing day ten years ago. The day my extended family came to visit....

"Pauline."

"Oh God," I thought, "here it comes."

"Be a pet and go make some tea for our visitors," continued my mom in her painstakingly perfected we-have-guests-so-for-the-next-couple-of-hours-we're-the-Cleavers tone.

"Who wants milk or sugar?" I mumbled as I begrudgingly got up from my seat.

Despite the obvious hardship of my mission to create the bottomless cup of tea, I was really a bit relieved to escape the confines of the den. It was only 2:00 P.M. on the day of our housewarming party, yet the pale afternoon sun was already having trouble penetrating the thickening layer of cigarette smoke that hung over our living room. My aunts and uncles seemed to pride themselves on their ability to function as human chimneys.

But secondhand smoke wasn't they only thing that was stifling me in there: I was being completely smothered with questions. *Did I like my new home? Had I any new friends? Did I miss the old ones?* And then there were the really fun questions. *Could I sing? After all, Uncle Sean's kids could sing. No? Why not? Every Mulleady was musically gifted. Did you know you take after your dad's side of the family? Too bad, your mom's side got the looks. Oh well, maybe in a few years.* My family seems to feel that a blood relationship is a license for brutal honesty. They were wrong, but I learned to cope.

What I despised most of all were questions about what had come to be called the "big move." They only reminded me of my parents' ultimate deception. A few short months before, my family and I had come from our home, Ireland, on a holiday to America. Little did I know at the time that our two-week vacation would stretch into a decade and counting. It seems my parents thought their itty-bitty white lie would save me a lot of messy good-byes. The fact was, leaving the country that up till then had been the only home I had ever really known had left me with a void and a longing in my heart for everything that was missing.

Speaking of everything that was missing, where were the damn tea bags? It had been all of ten minutes since my family's last round of the stuff, and if I didn't get some more tea into these people quickly, I was sure I would start seeing serious withdrawal symptoms. Then, just as I was imagining where I would hide if *I* were a tea bag, my thoughts were interrupted. Like an animal sensing danger, my ears pricked up at the mention of my name out in the living room. Although our guests didn't know it, the walls in this house envied the density of shower curtains. I left the kettle to boil, crept closer to the kitchen door, and heard the words that would change my life.

My Uncle Sean was running his mouth again, this time not about the accomplishments of his own kids but about the lack thereof on my part. Seeing that I had left the room, Uncle Sean asked my parents for a candid answer as to how I was doing in school. My parents, also noting that I had left the room and forgetting for the moment the paper-thin walls, gave him that candid answer, supplying him and the rest of the room with a lengthy list of my most recent failed endeavors.

Confident that among the countless cousins, aunts, and uncles inside at least one would rush to my defense, I could hardly believe what followed. Apparently my uncles, aunts, and cousins had to a man, woman, and child pretty much written me off as a failure. Even my parents seemed to agree, although not as wholeheartedly as the others. After a few initial grunts and sighs and a couple of "Yes, I know's" and "You're right's," they kept pretty quiet. The entire family had essentially deemed me a delinquent, a poor child who had been too traumatized by my sudden and drastic upheaval ever truly to adjust. No doubt I would never do well in school and would always be a bit of a problem kid.

I was dumbfounded, at a total loss, and I was mad, really mad. But I didn't know whether I should be more upset because people thought I was stupid or because people felt sorry for me. Even though the chatter in the other room soon turned to a more festive subject, I heard not another word; I didn't need to, for instantly I understood what I had been doing. In just one second, a thousand wise men had whispered their brilliance in my ear, infusing my mind with a peaceful light and abolishing the darkness caused by my petty fears and animosities. It was clear what I had to do. I would show them all. I realized no one was being punished by my stubbornness except me, and it was time to prove what I was capable of.

I haven't looked back since. The trouble I had with spelling differences vanished when I assumed my title as one of the best spellers in Hudson County, New Jersey. My trials and tribulations with Mrs. Gorrin's long division completely dissolved in the triumph of my high school graduation with math honors. As for my (ahem) speech impediment, it certainly didn't impede me any as I went on to become a finalist in a statewide forensics competition. Moreover, my accomplishments don't and won't stop there. I'm still giving my relatives something to talk about, that's for sure.

When I look back, I find it amazing that so insignificant an event could have so profound an impact on my life, that so trivial an incident should send so unwavering a determination coursing through my veins. Yet that is the definition of an epiphany, a moment of awakening. I'm sure I would eventually have caught on to my mistakes, but who knows how long it would have taken or what kind of person I would have been or even what my family relationships would have been like after all those years of failure—failures I would no doubt have blamed on my parents.

Even with all the changes in the past ten years, one thing did stay the same: my family was wrong—about lying, about the move, and about making up for that lie with brutal honesty in other areas. Most important, they were wrong about my being a delinquent, but that's okay, because I've learned to cope just fine, thank you very much!

Part Two

Argument and Persuasion

A Sadly Accepted Test

Erik Classon

"I'm so scared! What if I didn't break a thousand? I won't get into my college! I won't be able to pursue the career I wanted to!"

These are common fears of high school seniors across the nation. Their fears are not imaginary. Students can unfortunately be "made" or "broken" by their SAT (Scholastic Aptitude Test) scores. A student can be accepted or turned down by a university solely because her or his SAT scores meet or don't meet the established minimums. Is there a certain danger inherent in putting so much emphasis on one test? Does the test measure intelligence or the ability to make educated guesses?

The SAT, for all those who have not recently been put through the experience, is a standardized test. It consists of seven sections that measure both math and verbal skills. (One of the sections is experimental and is not counted toward the taker's score.) The mathematics portion of the test includes algebra, geometry, and various numeric "puzzles." The verbal section consists of analogies, filling in the blanks, synonyms, antonyms, and critical reading. The test is completely multiple choice, with the exception of the open-ended mathematical questions, which demand a number rather than A, B, C, D, or E. The SATs are scored on a numeric scale ranging from 200 to 1600. Math and verbal each count for 800 points. The test is to be completed in approximately three hours, depending on the efficiency of the proctor. In its physical state, this is all the SAT is, the actual pages, but American society has made it much more than that. Everyone who takes the test receives a permanent label that will last forever as a kind of identification.

As a college freshman, my encounter with the SAT wasn't that long ago. I have taken the pre-SAT, completed a high school preparatory course, gone through a tedious and expensive review course, and taken the test three times.

The first time I took the SAT was at the end of sophomore year. I, like many others, walked into the testing room with no idea of what to expect, and I took the test as best I could. I tried to answer every question and did not take any special notice of the overall structure of the test. I took the test in such an "unprepared" manner in order to find out how well I could do without being coached. I didn't believe people should have to be coached in order to attain an "accurate" score. I received my score/label approximately one month later: a 1030, not horrible but not wonderful either. The national average is approximately 1000, but my siblings received "above average" scores and therefore there was great pressure for me to do the same. My mother consoled me: "Don't worry! You have two years to improve, and you can take that Princeton Review course like your brother and sister." There was some truth in what she said, but I didn't like the idea that my own aptitude was not enough for me to score well on the test. After all, Webster's does define aptitude as "natural ability." How can something natural be coached? And so began my personal battle with the SAT.

My junior-year schedule included a free class intended to help students with the SAT. My teacher showed me ways to manipulate the test, how to get the right answer without actually knowing it. For example, all the words in each column of the analogies have to be the same part of speech, and there are only certain relationships between the words (opposites, synonyms, one is part of the other, etc.). This didn't feel right to me. If the right answer can be arrived at in this way, how can the test actually measure a student's aptitude? But I completed this course and once again I registered for the test and once again test day rolled around. This time I walked into the test room with some new tactics, ways to "beat" the test. I felt slightly more confident this time than I did the first time. I had spent many hours practicing and learning what to expect. When my scores arrived, I opened them with more trepidation than before. Although I received an 1130, which was an improvement, I still wasn't content: most highly competitive schools require their applicants to have a minimum of 1200 in order to be accepted. I still had time to improve my score some more, but I was beginning to wonder whether I was one of those students labeled "sub-1200." Maybe I wasn't destined to go to one of the more competitive colleges.

The people with the Princeton Review disagreed; they guaranteed that my score would increase by at least 100 points. This was the answer! I could finally attain that *stellar* score I so desired, and the best part was that it was guaranteed. How could I go wrong? I signed up for the Princeton Review home-tutoring course during the summer before my senior year. I could use the entire summer to get the tactics down. There was no way that test could get the best of me the third time around.

I adamantly did all of my assignments, studied my vocabulary, and did everything else my tutors told me to do. When the course was over my tutors told me I was well prepared and there was no reason I shouldn't do well. I was a little more skeptical, knowing my past, but I must admit, this time I felt really well prepared. I was going to "nail" that test.

I walked into the test room for the final time, all the techniques and tactics my tutors had showed me fresh in my mind. I felt extremely confident. Afterward I anxiously awaited my scores; I dearly wanted to find out what I got, but at the same time I would rather have never known. The day of judgment finally arrived; my mother told me that there was a letter from the College Board. This could only mean one thing! It was do or die! With trembling fingers I opened the letter. Slowly I pulled the piece of paper out of the envelope; I had gotten a 700 verbal and a 720 math! I jumped for joy. I breathed a sigh of relief. My life was saved. I would no longer have to worry about my future. The Educational Testing Service (ETS) had finally deemed me worthy of being a productive member of society.

The fact that students feel this way about one test shows there is something wrong with our method of evaluation. A current classmate of mine, Michael G., told me, "I can't believe that I, an honor student, top of the class, active during instruction, got a 1290 on the SAT. One of my friends, on the other hand, who does nothing during instruction, is not particularly intellectual, and has very poor grades, received a 1500." Michael's experience exemplifies how the SAT can shortchange a student who does not test well yet has the ability and solid character needed to be successful in college. I decided that the best way to find out how much emphasis is put on the test by colleges was to speak with someone who had firsthand information.

I asked Jane Crowley, an admissions officer at Boston College, how heavily the test weighs in the admission decision. She replied that it is the second most important criterion. She also revealed, "The SATs become more important as students get more competitive; it is a way to numerically rate the students whose transcripts are all very similar." A new and interesting thing I learned is the correlation between students who do well at college and students who take SAT preparatory courses. Crowley said, "The students who take these courses are concerned and hard-working, meaning they will work equally hard when they arrive at college. It is a fairly accurate indicator of how students will do."

But David Owen, an accomplished writer and a writing professor at Colorado College, feels there are some flaws with the SAT. In his essay "How They Write the SAT," he brings up many policies of the ETS that are rather alarming and further deflate the validity of the SAT. He begins this essay by stating, "Standardized multiple-choice tests, such as the Scholastic Aptitude Test, are more than hurdles on the way to college. The tests have become a pervasive measure of worthiness in our society—even a status symbol, as in, 'My boy scored double 700s' " (459). Clearly, there is a social status and "label" that comes along with one's SAT score. Their SAT score is something most people never forget. I would have had that 1400 stamped on my forehead.

Owen reveals the key to doing well on tests: "Understand how the test-makers think" (460). The way the ETS test-makers think, according to Owen, is to make the questions as "drab, humorless, and plodding" (460) as possible. A student who reads further into a question than the writer of the question intended will be penalized for it. The first time I took the test I didn't know this and received a much lower score than the one I "attained" after having been coached. Owen gives a sample question (translated from a French version of the test) that demonstrates how bright students may possibly get a wrong answer simply by applying the question to real life:

> 2. A customer is seated in a fancy restaurant. The clumsy waiter spills soup in his lap. The customer exclaims: *(A)* You could not pay attention, no? *(B)* The soup is delicious! *(C)* What good service! *(D)* I would like a spoon! (460)

Owen feels that B, C, and D are the kinds of comments he would make in this situation and that many students feel this way too, but they must realize that the ETS wants the "best" answer. "Thus bright students sometimes have trouble on ETS tests," Owen states, "because they see possibilities that ETS's question-writers missed. The advice traditionally given to such students is to take the test quickly and without thinking too hard" (460). I find it preposterous that a test intended to measure the aptitude (natural ability) of our college-bound youth encourages them not to think too hard.

A summer elapsed between the second and third time I took the test. The only thing I learned that summer was how to *take* the test, through the Princeton Review course. The tutors did not *teach* me English or mathematics, they simply taught me how to get the right answers. I am fairly certain that my aptitude (natural ability) did not make any great leaps during that time period; however, the ETS felt my aptitude was worth 380 more points. The first two times I took the test, I tried to answer the questions in the context of real life. The Princeton Review effectively numbed my mind against using my own opinions or considering what is really true. I thought of what the test-maker intended and answered accordingly. The test therefore measured my ability to see what the test-maker wanted, not my aptitude.

Owen goes on to show how the writers of the SAT connive to trick the test taker rather than find out whether or not he or she actually understands. He uses another sample question, in which the test taker is supposed to find the antonym of the word in question, as an example:

  4.   BYPASS: (A) enlarge (B) advance (C) copy (D) throw
       away (E) go through

One ETS reviewer "suggested substituting the word 'clog' for one of the incorrect choices (called 'distracters' in testing jargon), because 'perhaps clog would tempt the medicine freaks.' In other words, if the item were worded a little differently, more future physicians might be tempted to answer it incorrectly. The . . . comment is revealing of the level at which ETS analyzes their test" (461). Owen feels the emphasis of the test-makers is to make sure their answers can be defended. It doesn't matter if the answer is good or correct. The design of a test that will label people for the rest of their academic life would appear to be something that should be more carefully scrutinized; the answers should be universally agreed on.

Some people, myself included, argue that there are no "universal" answers, that everything is in a state of change, and that therefore the SAT cannot be very exact. In that case, it should be more relenting, allowing more than one answer per question. A test with as much importance as this one should model the dynamic nature of real life, not reduce everything to "either or." Real life is always a case of "more or less." The best way to write this kind of test is to allow free responses in which the student can explain his or her reasoning. Grading these tests would be much more difficult and time-consuming, because each test would require personal attention. But a standardized test should be nothing if not fair.

The SAT is a tradition most people are reluctant to question, because we feel the need for a label. But the SAT cannot remain static in our dynamic world. If there is to be a "standard scholastic aptitude test" / "standard natural ability test," then that is what it should measure, not who is willing to get the most coaching or spend the most money. If it needs to be revised and rethought, so be it. If it needs to be completely revamped, so be it. The test must do justice to the students who take it. In the world in which we live, much of our worth is determined by test scores and grades. Perhaps the flaws in our system of testing as a determinant of worth are so deeply ingrained that it is impossible to fix them without destroying the entire framework. No matter! It is time we begin to question this blind tradition.

Work Cited

Owen, David. "How They Write the SAT." In *The HarperCollins Guide to Writing*, 459–66. New York: HarperCollins, 1993.

People Cited

Crowley, Jane. Interview. November 5, 1997.

G., Michael. Interview. November 2, 1997.

Sex, Shots n' Academia

Maggie Messitt

❧

Boston College is known across the country as one of the most select universities to attend; it upholds the pride and educational values of the Jesuit tradition. But this small private college, with its annual price tag of approximately twenty-eight thousand dollars, has a reputation for more than a quality education. It is not surprising to flip through the pages of Princeton Review's *310 Best Colleges* and find that the listing under the category "What's Hot at Boston College" includes sex, alcohol, and academia. Even*Playboy* magazine once ranked BC as the "top party school in the country." Just follow the music and the crowds to BC's senior mods. Walk through the first open door you see and soak in the atmosphere. Steaming bodies crammed together, dancing and singing to the best tunes and laughing with friends. As the night goes on, clutching hands are everywhere and casual "hookups" somehow arrange themselves. Sit back and observe just a portion of the 5.5 million dollars U.S. college students spend annually on alcohol disappear down students' throats. Can after can, bottle after bottle, and who can miss those red "Solo" plastic cups littering every empty surface, filling up the countertops. With every passing minute, the awkward bodies that fill the sweltering room become more and more disoriented. Unfortunately, the fun and excitement do not lead most in the right direction.

Students end up in every possible situation. Imagine finding yourself, naked, in the middle of a mod, surrounded by strangers. Picture yourself lying face down in your own vomit, unconscious. What can you do when someone is taking advantage of you, if you're passed out drunk? And did you ever think you might flunk out of school? These are just a few unplanned results of consuming alcohol beyond one's limit. The two most serious problems directly or indirectly caused by alcohol at Boston College and other universities are sexual assault and academic failure.

Boston College's "random hookup" tradition is alive and well and going strong. "I accomplished my mission for the night! To hookup, of course," cheered a female freshman as she woke up with a big smile on her face, "but can you believe [my roommate] hooked up with three people in one night?!" Boston College parties are notorious for sexual advances and follow-throughs, especially when alcohol is present. The sexual activity of students on "The Heights" is way above average.

This winter I realized for the first time exactly what too much alcohol can do to my evening. I have never been a big drinker. I usually hold on to a glass that lasts me the entire evening. But for some reason, that night was different. I listened to a stranger with dimples who saw to it that I always had a full glass. Caught up in the party, I didn't realize the number of times he switched my glass. I wasn't aware of how much alcohol was in my body until I walked into the bathroom with a friend of mine. I stood uneasily as the tiles spun around me.

"Just lie here," he said, "please." A shiver ran through her body when she realized what was happening. He slid his hands down her sides as he whispered, "Just let me hold you in my arms." She lay there, not knowing what to do, her words frozen. His rehearsed lines and smooth moves made her feel so gross. A breeze from the partially ajar window created a chill. The room was so dark. The lights outside the plex shone through the window, scattering beams on the foreign walls. Peering across the room, she caught a reflection of the time in the mirror: 5:41. She had to get out of here. She wanted to get out of here . . . now.

She saw her boots lying on the floor not far from the bed. She slid from his hands and said, "I have to go." Grabbing her boots she walked out into the kitchen and quickly laced up. He walked out of his room and knelt down in front of her. He slid his hands up her legs and peered straight into her eyes. "Stay."

"I have to be up early," she muttered.

"I'll make sure you're up." He spoke imperiously.

"I need things from my room."

"I'll walk you there in the morning."

She felt so dirty. Looking down, she said, "No, I have to get home."

He insisted on walking her to her dorm. They trekked through the snow in silence. With each step, her heart beat faster and filled with embarrassment. The walk from lower campus to upper had never seemed so long. All that went through her head was a wish to wipe away the last six hours. She wished they had never happened.

Some women walk away from a night of heavy drinking without any real harm done, but others are not so lucky. The most common crime on college campuses today is rape. One out of every four college women has been raped or will have been raped before she completes her four years of schooling (National Victim Center 1992). After a few drinks, the average woman becomes too intoxicated to realize what's going on or to fend off unwanted sexual advances. A smile can be translated as a come-on. If he sees one thing and she means another, when and where does flirtation stop and sexual activity begin? When asked, several male BC freshmen said they did not believe sexual contact was a smart idea when alcohol was involved yet admitted that random hookups occurred at Boston College more often than not.

Leaning up against a wall, you catch a glance from that guy you've been eyeing for the past few weeks. He's ignored you all night, but now he seems to be flirting from a distance. Thanking your friend for the refill she hands you, foam brimming over the sides, you walk toward him. Slightly off-balance, you reach out and grab hold of a stranger's arm; you smile and continue on. Crossing the room, eyes dancing, it's hard to focus, but you say to yourself, "I'm fine, no problem. I'm buzzin', but I'm in control." Turning to talk to a friend, you feel the sudden cling of arms around your waist. A familiar voice whispers in your ear . . .

"Beer goggles! It's the only explanation." According to Robert, a BC student, "It seems to be that the more you drink, the more less-good-looking people become better looking," which seems to be the general consensus of the male population on campus. "Alcohol increases one's sex drive," comments a BC freshman named Brad; his roommates join in, in unison, "Beer makes you horny!"

In a study of college students, one in twelve males surveyed had committed acts that met the definition of rape. Furthermore, 84 percent of those men believed what they had done was definitely not rape (National Victim Center 1992). On BC's campus, three out of seven male students interviewed admitted that they have pushed others to drink so they would be unable to resist physical or emotional pressure to have sex. "Be wary of guys giving you free alcohol! If a guy keeps pouring free vodka down your throat, it's not necessarily benevolent . . . he's trying to get you drunk enough . . . to go home with him" ("Alcohol"). Seventy percent of student rapes are related to alcohol use, and 415 rapes take place among college students each day (Date Rape Statistics). Despite its frequent occurrence on college campuses, rape among students is almost never reported.

The second-largest problem spawned by alcohol abuse on college campuses—academic failure—can also be devastating. With the unofficial start of the weekend on Thursdays, attendance at Friday classes drops to a low: 'I don't like it, but I can guarantee that a portion of my students will be absent for classes held before 10 A.M., especially if they fall on Friday," comments one BC professor. Students with hangovers are often in no shape to be in class. But there is no place and no time in college to get behind, and once you do you will never catch up. It's a fact of life: when students start to drink heavily, they have problems keeping up with their work and are likely to start skipping classes. According to a recent Harvard study, 45 percent of college drinkers miss class as a result of their alcohol consumption, although only 35 percent admit to falling behind in their work because of their drinking.

"I began to turn the other cheek when it came to schoolwork. I can recall one week when my options were to study for a bio test and finish two papers or go out to The Office [a bar] with some of the guys. Needless to say, the choice was obvious to me: I'm headin' out! My grades suffered and I risked flunking four out of five of my classes. I had a serious wake-up call when my father threatened to stop paying my tuition" ("Binge Drinking").

Forty-one percent of all academic problems stem from alcohol abuse. Studies reveal that on the average, 7 percent of all college freshman drop out of school for alcohol-related reasons ("Binge Drinking"). Boston College administrators, take note: Imagine losing 196 students from the freshman class as the result of problems stemming directly and indirectly from alcohol. Calculate the lost tuition for the remaining three years, multiplied by the number of students. The university would lose approximately 16.5 million dollars, to say nothing of what happens to those students' lives.

It's a typical Friday night at Boston College. Parties are in the works, beers are on ice, the hard stuff is waiting on the makeshift bar. What each student decides to do is up to him or her, of course, but the decision many of them make becomes clear when you consider that 430 million gallons of alcohol are consumed by college students each school year. That's enough to fill an Olympic-sized swimming pool for every university ("Guide"). Unfortunately, when students dive in for a night of fun, they come away with much more than just a buzz. Whether you attend Boston College or any other university, drinking affects you for more than just the evening. Every time you grab a drink, you lose a bit of control over what happens to the rest of your night—and your life. Every time you return to the keg, your odds for disaster increase. Both students and the administration need to realize that there is a problem with alcohol at universities such as Boston College and that the related effects—sexual mistakes and academic failure primary among them—are going to destroy the students in the long run.

Works Cited

Alcohol and Acquaintance Rape: Strategies to Protect Yourself and Each Other.
Pamphlet. Higher Education

Center for Alcohol and Other Drug Prevention, 1997. Available on-line at:
http: //www. med. unc. edu/alcohol/prevention/rape.html

The 310 Best Colleges, 82–83. New York: Princeton Review Publications,
1997.

"Binge Drinking on Campus: Results of a National Study." On-line.
Available at: http://www.edc.org/hecpubs/binge.htm

Date Rape Statistics. On-line. Available at:
http://www.cs.utk.edu/bartley/sa/stats.html

"The Guide to College Drinking." On-line. Available at:
http://www.glness.com

National Victim Center Statistics, April 23, 1992. On-line. Available at:
http://pubweb.ucdavis.edu/Documents/RPEP/nvcstats.htm

Do You Hear the Stereotype?

Kelly Miller

Students might expect a guide to drinking to be about how to tap a keg, where to buy the cheapest case, and what's good for curing hangovers. After all, many people think college is just a four-year party with a $20,000 cover charge—and their favorite class is Partying and Drinking 101.

—Internet information

How do you feel now? You have just become the victim of a ferocious stereotype that is sweeping our nation. This kind of generalization is gaining popularity as more studies examine college drinking habits. Numbers and percent signs are stripping the average student of the image he or she deserves: the image of the maturing adult. College students across the nation are being categorized as irresponsible delinquents with a drinking problem. So, Delinquent, are you going to let this stereotype undermine your college years?

In a 1990 survey of attitudes and characteristics of college freshmen, approximately 52 percent of those responding self-reported having had a beer in the past year ("Alcohol" 22). Average consumption ranged from five to seven drinks per week. Forty-four percent reported binge drinking (consumption of five or more drinks in one sitting) within the two weeks prior to the study (21). This group is seven to ten times more likely than nonbinge drinkers or infrequent drinkers to be involved in problems such as injury, property damage, unwanted sex, or trouble with the police. According to these statistics, there is a 52 percent chance that you have consumed alcoholic beverages and a 44 percent chance that you have engaged in binge drinking. But now let's turn these figures around. There is a 48 percent chance that you do not drink and an even greater chance—56 percent—that you are not a binge drinker. These numbers indicate that over half of college freshman are not binge drinkers and are therefore undeserving of a stereotype attributing such behavior to them.

The rising popularity of drug-, alcohol-, and tobacco-free dormitories illustrates the reality behind these phenomenal numbers. A growing number of students are choosing to reside in substance-free housing. At the University of Maryland, about 120 freshmen moved into special substance-free housing in 1993 when the program was first offered. Three years later (1996) the number of students living in substance-free dormitories had risen to about 1,000 of a total of 8,000 on-campus residents. The option was extended to meet the demands of the upperclassmen as well. This tremendous increase in life-style preference is not limited to Maryland. The phenomenon has also manifested itself at the University of Michigan; Vassar College, in Poughkeepsie, NY; Washington University, in St. Louis, MO; the Rochester (NY) Institute of Technology, and dozens of other colleges throughout the nation. Students want clean environments as well as clean lifestyles (Shen A1).

The stigma that has been placed on college students nationwide is false and misleading. Not all college students engage in binge drinking and therefore not all college students should be treated as binge drinkers. The contradiction present in this image is immense. It is quite ironic that the primary goal of a college student is to become a more learned individual, yet the image often associated with a college student is that of the reckless drunken ignoramus who is incapable of sagacious thought.

Sadly, this image is not entirely false, as I am the first to acknowledge. There are individuals whose knowledge of physical science deals more with exactly how long it will take them to get drunk if the alcohol is consumed upside down through a funnel than with the evolution of the inclined plane. However, there are more individuals (56 percent of college freshman) who choose not to participate in this life-style. These students may drink occasionally in moderation, but they are able to recognize their own limits and do not allow alcohol to alter their primary reason for attending college: to think and act intelligently. These students are serious about furthering their education and do not deserve the detestable image so often assigned them.

Recently I visited South Padre Island, Texas, on spring break. South Padre Island is a popular spot for "Spring Breakers." True, a fine display of wild college drinking did take place, and many of the students were there for this purpose. Students were seen participating in activities unimaginable to most, and most of those able to imagine these activities would prefer not to. Among this rowdy bunch, however, there is a percentage that is significantly tamer. This population coexists with the barbarous members, but they are not part of that life-style. My friends and I traveled to South Padre for our spring break because we wanted to go to an affordable warm spot where the three of us could spend time together. We wanted to have a good time in a setting conducive to a laid-back, carefree vacation. The problem in Padre was with the older members of society. They put all college students into the ruffian stereotype and failed to recognize that some of us do have self-control.

My friends and I were treated poorly by the hotel staff because of this stereotype. When we returned to our room after our first outing, we found that our coffee maker, glasses, and ice bucket had been taken away by housekeeping. When we asked why, we were told it was so that we would not break them. I can understand the concerns of the staff; however, we were paying the same rate as their "more civil" customers, and more important, we are intelligent beings, not irrational beasts. Despite the "Spring Breaker" designation so often applied to us, we had no intention of destroying hotel property. It was in South Padre that I first heard the blare of the stereotype I had previously been deaf to.

As college students, we are working toward degrees that will land us professional careers. Soon these older members of society will be trusting us with far more than their coffee makers, glasses, and ice buckets; we will be running their businesses, teaching their children, even curing their illnesses. It is not right to burden such a diverse group with such a stereotype when it is only a small percentage that deserves the stereotype and all it implies. True, the percentage of binge drinkers on South Padre Island during spring break is much greater than the percentage of binge drinkers on the average college campus, but that does not excuse this display of discriminatory behavior. The percentage of nonbinge drinkers is still deserving of respect.

Another concern I have regarding this issue is the effect the stereotype is having on the way we see ourselves as college students. I was disturbed after reading an essay written by one of my classmates. In her observation of an on-campus party she said: "I was also surprised to realize that all of the typical stereotypes of college kids at parties are correct. They drink, get sick, flirt, play games, and listen to loud (deafening) music. I could agree that if you aren't in college, you might think that all those things aren't fun or you can't understand why we all love to go to this sort of illegal gathering." Is this really how we view ourselves? This is not my idea of a fun weekend. The college experience, including the parties, is supposed to be at least somewhat enjoyable and maybe even pleasant. As astonishing as this may sound, I do not feel that getting sick while listening to deafening music is a good time.

Certain that I was not the only one who shared this opinion, I conducted a survey on the drinking habits and opinions of my peers. I chose twenty-five random Boston College students as my subjects and asked them (1) if they considered themselves a binge drinker and (2) if they had ever gone an entire week without consuming alcohol. Of the twenty-five students surveyed, only three considered themselves binge drinkers according to the definition of a binge drinker. And—a pleasant surprise—all twenty-five reported they had gone an entire week without consuming alcohol. Several students even reported that they enjoy not drinking.

This survey of average Boston College students reinforces my belief that not all college students are binge drinkers. The fact that some students actually enjoy not drinking furthers my opinion that we, as college students, are sick of the stereotype applied to us. We want to prove that we deserve better. There is so much more to college than getting sick in strange places and waking up with a hangover. In Boston alone there is a wide variety of theatres, dance clubs, and sporting events to attend. There are plenty of on-campus events to take part in as well, such as student comedy troops, on-campus movie showings, and campus parties. Don't get me wrong, I love parties just as much as any other student. Partying is a great way to meet people and have fun as long as you are able to recognize your limit and drink responsibly. Waking up in a pool of vomit next to someone you hardly know is a bad experience.

College is a wonderful mixture of development, achievement, experience, and good times. Who wants to spoil these four years by bolstering a stereotype that is false to begin with? If you have decided that you have heard enough of this stereotype, then join with other college students across the nation and show how intelligent you really are. Prove to those who believe this stereotype that college students are not ignoramuses and that the $20,000+ cover charge provides us with more than a bracelet allowing us to drink.

Works Cited

Gorman, Christine. "Higher Education: Crocked on Campus." *Time* (domestic edition), December 19, 1994. Available on-line at: http.//www.pathfinder.com/time/magazine/archive/1994/941219.health.html

Shea, Christopher. "New Look at College Drinking." *Chronicle of Higher Education* 41 (1994): A39

Shen, Fern. "These Dorm Rooms: A Study in Sobriety." *The Washington Post*, September 3, 1996, Al+.

Wechsler, Henry. "Alcohol and the American College Campus: A Report from the Harvard School of Public Health." *Change* 28 (1996): 20—25.

————."Health and Behavioral Consequences of Binge Drinking in College." *Journal of the American Medical Association*, December 7, 1994, 1672–77.

"Welcome to Drinking: A Student's Guide." On-line. Available at: http://www.glness.com/ndhs

The *Veritas* About Maroon

Brock Daniels

❦

If you look quickly, you may mistake the maroon of Boston College for the crimson of Harvard. Spend a day at each place and your mistake will become obvious rather quickly, somewhere around the speed of light—a physical constant I'm sure nearly every person I observed during my day at Harvard could regurgitate for me (299,792,458 meters per second, in case you were wondering) But I'm not going to be so picky. I'm not going to focus on the difference in what respective "students," and I use that word cautiously, know. I once met a kid who had memorized the value for pi to one-hundred-and-some-odd decimal places, which I find no more valuable than knowing the right liquor store to get the cheapest six- pack of Bud. The issues I have concern the polarity of attitudes between two schools such as Harvard and Boston College, and, specifically, the attitudes of "students" toward learning in general.

It must be noted that this essay is based only on my limited, albeit thorough, observations. In the face of this admitted sampling error, it's hard for me to be entirely firm in my statements, even in my own mind. I know full well that there are exceptions; but in the same breath, I have to admit that certain glaring disparities are undeniable. First, a mild comparison of events I witnessed on successive days.

While on one of my innumerable trips on the lovely Newton bus around BC's campus, I overheard a conversation impossible to ignore. It proceeded as follows:

"You going to class?" The query came from a blonde girl clad in typical BC garb, a white T-shirt and black slacks. Her question stirred some life in her friend, who had been, up to this point, staring out the window at the beautiful March day as we headed toward main campus.

47

"I don't know, it's so nice out. We could just go back and, like, lay out," she replied, stretching her arms wide (unlike those of the other passengers, they weren't inhibited by the weight of books or notebooks). "But I didn't get up for the exam yesterday so maybe I should go."

"Again?" her friend asked in a not-so-astonished voice. She turned her head, causing her golden hair to flop over her shoulders. "What'd you have?"

"Chem. It was like quarter to nine and my alarm went off and I just put my pillow over my head and went back to bed." She patted down her teenage uniform, jeans and a GAP T-shirt, in search of something. "Doesn't matter, I, like, would've failed it anyway, so why bother? You got a cigarette?"

Am I alone in perceiving the disturbing nature of this conversation? An exam is something you might want to get up for, regardless of how "tired" you are. It would have been one thing if it were one of those there-was-a-power-outage-and-the-backup-batteries-died-and-my-alarm-didn't-go-off situations, but this was more I-was-too-hung-over-to-get-up-and-go-to-class. And it gets worse. The conversation progressed from what are you doing this weekend (note: this is a Tuesday; extra note: the weekend begins on Thursday, assuming there was an end to the previous weekend) to what did you do last weekend to who's buying for you to that new-English form of good-bye, give-me-a-call-if-you're-going-out. Such conversations are so typical I won't bother to transcribe the specifics—if you have the uncontrollable urge to overhear one, get on any BC bus any day of the week at any time of day and I can guarantee you'll encounter one. Wait. I feel compelled to share one brief aside:

The original interrogator pointed out the window:

"What's that?"

Her companion, still pondering the absence of her cigarette, answered questioningly, "Oh, that's the Charles River, isn't it?"

"Yeah, that's right."

What's wrong with that? you ask. Well, I suppose it's a valid question for a freshman, even though, if you remember, this conversation occurred in mid-March. For those of you who aren't familiar with the bus routes at BC, the bus leaves the lower campus stop and circles around the perimeter of the campus, passing alongside the city reservoir—the very same body of water to which the freshman who posed the question was pointing. So, let's compare: Charles River, the operative word being river, and city reservoir. Hmmm . . . reservoir = lake = body of water surrounded by land on *all* sides; and, last time I checked, river = flowing body of water surrounded by land on *only two* sides. Therefore it is only logical that reservoir = river and that city reservoir = Charles River, right? Ummm . . . no, sorry, please play again.

This is a facetious point at best but still relevant. Mistaking one lake for another is one thing and understandable. Mistaking a lake for a river is quite another—it shows a lack of simple logical reasoning, of just plain thinking. The same is applicable for not getting up for a test. Isn't thirty points "earned" by writing down equations (which most people cheatingly store in their graphing calculators anyway) for a few problems slightly better than a zero? Does it take a lot of effort to get up, get on a bus, go to class, take the fifty-minute test and go home back to a not-yet-cold bed? Does it take that much effort to think? The amount of intelligence required to think through the little river/reservoir line of reasoning is certainly less than the hours spent agonizing over who one can find to buy beer. Conclusion: it's all a matter of choice.

In contrast, I walk across the campus of Harvard and hear conversations about the theatre performance last night, Washington politics, and whatever the lecture topic was in class today (a class that has actually been gotten up for and attended). It seems almost foreign to me now, as I approach the end of my freshman year, to pause outside Harvard's science building and listen to a group of people stand around for over an hour discussing their recent E-chem class. These are not people sporting pocket-protectors, starched shirts, and plastic-framed glasses holding lenses capable of focusing the sun into a laser beam. These are normal people. There is an air about the place that epitomizes the ideal of higher learning; the campus itself is conducive to reading. I can go there to read for hours, whereas at Boston College I have to search for hours just to find a quiet place away from the constant refrains of "where's the party?" "who drank the most?" and "who hooked up with whom?" The monotony of such worthless conversations is mind-numbing.

It is not, though, the fault of the institution. The requirements of BC's classes are not much different from, and the caliber of BC's faculty is roughly the same as, that of any Ivy League university. Boston College is ranked thirty-eighth in the nation out of over one thousand schools; the problem is not inherent. I could argue it is the fault of the admissions committee and the students they select each year for the freshman class, but even while that is plausible, it is impossible to place the blame there. The board can admit candidates only from among the applications received. It is not the university, the faculty, or the admissions committee—it is the "students" and their *choice* of attitudes.

I find that the majority of people at BC avoid "nonrequired reading" like the plague. I quote, "You're reading for fun? Man, we need to get you a VCR." "Reading for fun" is something reserved for geeks/nerds/losers, choose your term of derogation . . . wait, am I a freshmen in college or in high school? Sometimes it's hard to tell the difference. Small, isolated incidents like these form the foundation of what is a very frightening social structure. It does not take a theoretical mind to extrapolate the rest of what must go on, the reality present here. There's nothing wrong with partying, drinking, having fun—they're all a part of college life. And I know for a fact it's a part of Harvard and every other school—but such things have their place. When you wake up on Tuesday morning with a hangover, it might be time to reassess your priorities.

As my freshmen year draws to a close, I find it hard to believe I don't have to remove my socks to count the number of intelligent in-class conversations I've been involved in. And I can't even begin to count the number of non-beer-related conversations I've witnessed outside the classroom . . . no, seriously, I can't. I can't because I don't recall a single such conversation with which to begin counting. The worst part is, this is a highly contagious epidemic: the three people out of a class of forty who have something to say will remain silent because they are either, one, too shy, or two, understand that their efforts will be in vain. The professor presenting a point and two people responding (generally quoting what they have read the night before) to his puppy-dog questions formulated to evoke a predetermined response does not constitute a class discussion. Admittedly, I fall into the latter of the two aforementioned categories and in that respect I'm part of the problem. But it isn't easy to debate a point amid the snores emanating from those who actually rolled into class and the snickering from the "back- row dwellers" who don't understand the question but find it uncontrollably hilarious that the professor said "cucumber."

If Harvard is conducive to reading, what is BC's environment conducive to? What can be done about this? *Should* anything be done? I haven't any answers, nor am I looking for them any longer—I certainly don't expect to have a class discussion about it anytime soon. And let me note that this is not a persuasive essay but in fact something more akin to an acceptance letter. I will admit to my naiveté. This is not what I expected college to be like in the least. I never could have imagined my high school multiplied by a factor of forty, soaked in ten times the amount of beer, and with a million times less responsibility, but here it is. Let's not even mention the fact that we're all paying $32,000 (subject to increase) a year for it. Four years ago, I was a freshman in high school, and four years later I'm still there—the math just doesn't add up.

Who Cares About Child Care?

Meghan O'Neill

❧

Since the 1970s, the number of families in which both parents of young children must work outside the home simply to make ends meet has steadily climbed. In some cases, other family members are able to watch these children. However, most of these families need outside child care that fits into their meager budget and yet provides proper supervision for their children. Unfortunately, good child care is hard to come by: very few facilities that can meet these standards are available in the United States. According to a recent *Newsweek* report, "Experts estimate that two thirds of child care arrangements are substandard" (Kantrowitz 63).

Undoubtedly, inadequate child care is responsible for many other problems as well. Many parents have been forced to work opposite shifts so that one parent can always be with the children. With such a schedule, the parents often have no time for each other; stresses like these often contribute to divorce. In 1976, in her sociological study, *Worlds of Pain*, author Lillian B. Rubin asserted, "Today more than ever before, family life has been impoverished for want of time, adding another threat to the already fragile bonds that hold families together" (xxxviii). More recently, in her book, *Value Judgments,* well-known *Boston Globe* columnist Ellen Goodman reported that "well over two million kids between the ages of five and thirteen are home alone every weekday afternoon" (284). Many communities try to offer after-school programs for these latchkey kids, but as with many other essential child-care services, not every community has the funds to create such a program.

Our current child-care system is scandalously inadequate; there are few facilities and few regulations governing those facilities. Some states require that day-care facilities be licensed, supposedly an assurance that basic health and safety requirements have been met. These licenses are not the most reliable, however, and individual attention is usually not given to the children in these facilities. By way of example, in Maine, Montana, and New York, the mandated adult-to-child ratio in a day-care room of six-year-olds (first graders) is one to ten. In the same room of rambunctious six-year-olds in Texas, the mandate is one to twenty-six (Seligson et al. 131).

In the face of this lack of an organized system of stringent regulations and one-on-one care, many parents seek to provide individual care in their homes. Although individual care is certainly the more desirable option, if parents are struggling to make ends meet there is little chance they will be able to afford an expensive, high-quality nanny. Some seize on the option of hiring an au pair—a teenager from a foreign country who helps with housework and baby-sitting while living in the family's home. Louise Woodward, an au pair in Newton, Massachusetts, was convicted of shaking to death the child she was entrusted to care for. Woodward, who was only seventeen when this happened, worked forty-five hours per week watching two small children, ages two and eight months.

How many seventeen-year-olds in the United States have jobs requiring a forty-five-hour work week? How many high school seniors are responsible enough to watch two infants simultaneously? The company that sent Woodward to the United States, EF Au Pair, gives its recruits minimal training: the teenagers are expected to be mother's helpers, not full-time nannies. The family Woodward resided with had approached her several times about her late nights and had asked her to observe a curfew, which she failed to do. It was obvious that the family not only was overworking Woodward but was unhappy with her as well (Rosenburg 61). The obvious question here is, why not simply hire someone else? The unfortunate reality is that in all likelihood, there was no one else available.

The tragic death of the infant in the Woodward case eloquently bespeaks the child-care crisis in our nation today. Parents should not be forced to turn to people like Woodward as an alternative to mediocre and expensive day care. Although the government, in documenting the increase in two-wage-earner families over several census periods, has tacitly acknowledged that they are now a necessity, it has not acknowledged the need to provide child care for these families, which seems to be the next logical step. In order to meet the needs of working parents, the United States government must provide a system of universal, affordable child care for its citizens with children. Federal regulation needs to be put in place. What is proper care for a child in New York must be equal to what is proper care for a child in Texas. If the cost of implementing such programs is too great a burden for a particular state, funds need to be allocated to help that state meet minimal requirements. There cannot be differing standards of care for American children.

In many nations, this kind of federal regulation does exist. When child care is a federally subsidized and government-regulated operation, it would be unheard of for a family to keep on a nanny whom they felt was inadequate: other options would be available. For example, according to Doctors Marsden and Mary Wagner, who back in 1976 conducted a study of the Danish National Child Care System, "day care, private and public, part day and all day, neighborhood and industrial, in private homes and public centers, from birth to eighteen years, has been in continuous operation" in Denmark since 1870 (68).

Politicians in the United States are quick to condemn television characters like Murphy Brown for contributing to the breakdown of family values, yet they cannot acknowledge the fact that something fixable is contributing significantly to this breakdown. Indeed, even when it became apparent that those in government were not immune, the problem was ignored. Zoe Baird and Kimba Wood were consecutive candidates for attorney general in 1993; both admitted to having hired illegal aliens to care for their children. In particular, Zoe Baird, the first candidate, caused a great stir among the American public for, as columnist Ellen Goodman quipped, she was "a mother who earned half a million bucks a year [but] still couldn't find child care" (218). Baird told the Senate Hearing Committee, "I was acting more as a mother than as someone who would be sitting here designated to be attorney general" (219). Although members of the working class inevitably have a more difficult time affording decent child care, mothers like Zoe Baird, with her huge salary, and parents like the ones in the Woodward case, who are both doctors, have the same problem. Regardless of a substantial income, many families still cannot find decent child care.

So how can this huge problem be fixed, specifically? Inevitably, the most favorable solution is not the cheapest, the simplest, nor the fastest to implement.

The solution I envision would be for the government to establish "junior colleges" for child-care training. The graduates of these schools would earn degrees attesting to their expertise, and the federal government would set minimum requirements for all child-care establishments concerning cleanliness, employee competence, and quality of overall care. Facilities would receive frequent inspections by government officials to make sure they were adhering to federal child-care standards and regulations. Any government-licensed child-care technician would be required to take a review course every few years (just like CPR) to go over the skills learned in school and to ensure responsibility and expertise in the field. With a series of government-established child-care facilities guaranteeing the graduates a job, attendance at these schools would certainly be enticing: after all, child care is not a waning field.

In order to make the schools more affordable, the government could set up scholarships for the students—paying a percentage of the tuition with the agreement that the child-care worker, upon graduation, would work off the loan at one of the government-subsidized child-care facilities.

A system like the one I have outlined has been long in place in Denmark. There, students looking for careers as caregivers in one of the nation's many day-care centers are required to take courses in child growth and development, child health, nutrition, child law, and play skills as part of the training program. The program lasts three years, and at the time of the Wagners' study, was in place at fourteen child-care training institutions (Wagner 75). And apparently, it works—*it has been in place for more than a hundred years*. Denmark is certainly much smaller than the United States, but considering our current standards of child care, it would be foolish not to attempt something to improve the situation.

I don't pretend that implementing this solution in our own country will not be expensive, but I certainly think its benefits outweigh its costs. Fewer parents will have to worry about where their kids are and whether they're okay. They will feel more secure entrusting their child to someone whom the government has fully endorsed. Improved child care will eliminate a major stress in many parents' lives, possibly saving many marriages.

Systems similar to this one have been successful around the world. Indeed, every piece of literature I researched on the subject was quick to point out that the United States is alone among developed nations in not having an organized system of national child care (Wagner 75).

The problem has been too long ignored. It is time for some government action and regulation. Recent administrations have been very concerned with the quality of education, which is certainly important, but what about the years before school or the hours after? While it is very important that we, as Americans, provide a solid foundation on which our children's future can be built, we also have to be concerned with the reality of child care. Every day after school two million kids sit home alone because their parents don't have, can't afford or cannot find a baby-sitter. Almost a year ago, a baby boy in Newton was killed while in the care of a very young and undertrained au pair. How many more horror stories do we have to hear before something is done?

Works Cited

Goodman, Ellen. *Value Judgments.* New York: Farrar Straus Giroux, 1993.

Howes, Carolee. "Child Outcomes of Child Care Programs." *Yearbook in Early Childhood Education: Issues in Child Care.* Ed. Bernard Spodak, et al. New York: Columbia University Press, 1992.

Kantrowitz, Barbara, et al. "Keeping Your Kids Safe." *Newsweek.* 10 November 1997: 60-63.

Rosenburg, Debra, and Evan Thomas. "'I Didn't Do Anything'." *Newsweek.* 10 November 1997: 60-63.

Rubin, Lillian B. *Worlds of Pain.* New York: Basic Books. 1976.

Seligson, Michelle, et al. "Before and After School Child Care." *Yearbook in Early Childhood Education: Issues in Child Care.* Ed. Bernard Spodak, et al. New York: Columbia University Press, 1992.

Wagner, Marsden, M.D., and Mary Wagner, Ph.D. *The Danish National Child Care System.* Boulder: Westview Press, 1976.

Part Three

Textual and Cultural Analysis

Your Opinion's Your Own, I Got Mine Too

Jeff Barlekamp

It's happened to me countless times. I'm having a pleasant conversation with a person I have just met. Everything is going fine until the question comes up.

"So what kind of music do you listen to?" the other person will ask nonchalantly. I hesitate for a moment and smile to myself, knowing the reaction that is coming.

"I listen to heavy metal, mostly." I await the widening of my newly found acquaintance's eyes or the look of shock on his or her face.

"Really? I never would have guessed it. You don't look to be . . . that type."

That type. What exactly is that type, anyway? I do not usually bother arguing. I just smile and nod in passive agreement. Then comes the next question.

"So . . . what do your parents think about you listening to that . . . stuff?"

"Actually, my dad introduced me to it."

Silence. Then, "Oh."

That first experience with heavy metal music took place when I was about twelve years old. I was sitting in the car with my father, stopped at a traffic light on a busy street in my hometown. Clicking on the cassette player, my father proceeded to pop in a tape by a group I later learned to be Black Sabbath, believed by many to have been the original heavy metal band (Weinstein 14). To this day I still remember the sounds of the blowing wind, rain, and chiming bells that echoed throughout my father's little automobile before the haunting rhythm of the opening track, appropriately titled "Black Sabbath," began. Soon everything suddenly quieted down. Supported by a mysterious, downright spooky bass line supplied by Geezer Butler, the voice of vocalist John "Ozzy" Osbourne kicked in. In an emotionally charged and deathly haunting tone, he sang his first, now legendary line: *What is this that stands before me?*

Even though I was in my own hometown on a beautiful, sunny day, sitting next to a man I trusted, I could not stop the chills running down my spine. For the first and only time in my life, I was scared by a song. As I overcame my initial fright, however, I realized the music I was listening to was amazing. I had never before heard such emotion come out of a guitar or a vocalist. It was quite beautiful and captivating. Was this the same heavy metal I had heard so many people laughing at and ridiculing? Sitting there listening to this incredible song, I found myself wondering two things: first, how my dad could possibly listen to such cool music, and, second, why such a phenomenal form of music was so blatantly ignored or mocked by so many people.

I'm not sure why people can never seem to get over the fact that I listen to and enjoy heavy metal music. Maybe it's because of the negative stereotypes often associated with the genre. Those who listen to it are often assumed to be poorly educated, apathetic, long-haired young males who are attracted to the music's dealings with "suicide, Satan, and crime" (Walser 180). People often find it hard to believe that someone like me, with short brown hair, a clean-shaven face, and a pretty decent level of intelligence, could listen to this same type of music. Through my example, I hope people will realize there can be a lot more involved with heavy metal than loud, noisy instruments and superficial lyrics.

Although the main instruments used in an average metal band are electric guitars, bass, and drums, all played at a high volume (Shuker 148), this does not mean that the songs are not melodic or creative. I must admit the lyrics can be very superficial at times, as in the song "Mainline," by the band Kiss:

> *You know that it's easy, so come on and please me, I want you*
> *I'm needin' some lovin', I'm hot like an oven, it's so true*

Most people fail to understand, however, that these lyrics are not intended to be taken seriously. Bands like Kiss are formed to provide entertainment and claim to offer nothing more. Most metal lyrics, however, particularly those of more contemporary songs, are very complex and poetic, while at the same time offering some intelligent reflections on life in general. For example, take the song "Across Vast Oceans," by a band called Mindrot:

We are longing, wishing, might be still for what it seems
That chains ring where the halls contained dreams
Like I, onward with grace, existing to love,
And to be free . . .

Although this form of poetic content is prevalent in most metal music to-day, a majority of people still hold on to the superficial stereotypes when they think of the genre in general (Shuker 147).

There must be some reason heavy metal music is the most disliked form of music around (Bryson 894). From personal experience, it seems that people may have heard one or two stereotypical, so-called metal songs in their lives, and quickly proceed to dismiss the entire genre as nothing more than crushing guitars and wailing vocals accompanied by sexist or "evil" lyrics. However, for me and for thousands of other fans all over the world, the music runs much deeper than that. It is in fact a complex, melodic form of music performed by very talented and accomplished musicians. Most of the lyrics are positive; only a few deal with negative issues, and "when they do, it is in ways more complex and sophisticated than [critics] recognize" (Hamm 369). The band Life of Agony, for example, can easily be dismissed as another group of young guys out there simply to complain about their problems; however, the lyrics to their song "Words and Music" show just how important heavy metal music is as a form of expression:

It may not be much
But this is all I got . . .
It's these words and music
That keeps me living, keeps me breathing

Heavy metal music is not only a way to release aggression but is also as an honest, sincere expression of discontent with a society that more often than not chooses to reject heavy metalers and their way of life.

When people need more of a justification for why I listen to metal than the fact that I like it, I let them know about the community of heavy metal fans and bands, which is simply nonexistent in many other types of music. Since metal is now so blatantly shunned by both radio and MTV (Weinstein 150), fans show their persistence and true love for their music by bonding with one another (Bryson 885) and by supporting their favorite bands by attending their concerts. The constant touring by metal bands to promote their music helps bring the musicians and their fans closer together than is possible with most other types of music (Hamm 223). Bands bond with their fans during these shows and encourage their fans to unite in their common interest in metal music. Since most of the outside world is out there to attack them, the bands say, it is vital that they stick together and do their best to keep their small yet audible voice alive.

I remember vividly the sights, sounds, and smells of my first metal concert. Seven bands and a few hundred fans were jammed into a tiny club no larger than the Devlin lecture hall. I was fifteen and deathly scared, since all I knew about these concerts was what I had heard on television or from other people. Supposedly, the concerts were dangerous, everyone there was a weirdo out to hurt you, and the bands were extremely loud and noisy. Well, it was loud, but everything else was false. Although some of the people there may not have looked "normal" or "nice," I discovered, from talking with them and sharing concert-going experiences, that they were decent people there only to enjoy the music along with fellow fans. Contrary to what I had been hearing for years, there were no Satan worshipers trying to recruit new followers, no people trying their best to injure me physically. There is no more violence at these shows than there was at "the opera in nineteenth century Paris, or at the performances of Shakespeare in nineteenth century New York" (Walser 181). For the first time, I realized that maybe, just maybe, heavy metal music had been given a bad rap.

After overcoming my initial fears, which had been triggered in me by other people, I started to go to these concerts regularly. I have since been to see metal bands with my father and my uncle, who also grew up listening to this type of music. It's a very interesting experience to see parents come in with their kids in tow and enjoy the show together. This form of community, one shared not only among fans but also among family members, is something that must be seen in order to be believed.

To this day, there is nothing more enjoyable for me than coming home after a long day, popping in one of my favorite metal CDs, flopping down on my bed, closing my eyes, and just listening. I am always amazed at the energy these musicians exhibit while blending protestation with intelligence, melody with aggression, and beauty with harshness to create a single emotion-laden tune. For this reason, I do my best to convince people of heavy metal's worth and true beauty as a form of self-expression. I know, however, that people will continue to pass heavy metal music off as a worthless "moron joke, fodder for frustrated teens and dominion of dim-witted devil worshipers" (Weinstein 2).

And they wonder why we're frustrated.

Works Cited

Biohazard. "Concerned." *State of the World Address.* Compact disc. Warner Brothers, 1994.

Black Sabbath. "Black Sabbath." *Black Sabbath.* Compact disc. Warner Brothers, 1970.

Bryson, Bethany. "'Anything but Heavy Metal': Symbolic Exclusion and Musical Dislikes." *American Sociological Review,* October 1996, 884–89.

Hamm, Charles. *Putting Popular Music in Its Place.* New York: Cambridge University Press, 1995.

Kiss. "Mainline." *Hotter Than Hell.* Compact disc. Casablanca 422-824147-2, 1974.

Life of Agony. "Words and Music." *River Runs Red.* Compact disc. Roadrunner 16861- 9043-2, 1993.

Mindrot. "Across Vast Oceans." *Dawning.* Compact disc. Relapse 81676-69252, 1995.

Shukur, Roy. *Understanding Popular Music.* New York: Routledge, 1994.

Walser, Robert. "Running With the Devil: Power, Gender, and Madness in Heavy Metal Music." Ph.D. Diss., University of Minnesota, 1991. Quoted in Hamm.

Weinstein, Deena. *Heavy Metal.* New York: Lexington, 1991.

Lifegaurding Against Baywatch

Shaina Vigue

❧

CJ, the pretty and popular blonde bombshell of Baywatch, has just started her day lifeguarding at the beach. It is early morning, and she spots a runner along the shoreline. The man is exhausted yet proceeds to go into the water and tries to swim out to the buoys. He hasn't been swimming for more than a few minutes before he begins to go under. CJ immediately runs to the rescue and hauls the swimmer out of the ocean, just in time to restart his breathing and save his life.

I hoist myself up the lifeguard-tower ladder toward the platform where my chair rests. The hot metal bars burn my hands as I climb. I look out into the clear blue water and try to concentrate on the swarm of people who are trying to escape the awful heat of the day. I keep scanning the pool, but honestly it feels ineffective. There are so many swimmers; it's impossible to keep track of them all. Only fifteen minutes have elapsed since the beginning of my shift but already it feels like an eternity.

Mitch, the head lifeguard of the beach, is at Baywatch headquarters. His son, Hobie, comes by to say hi to his Dad and decides to take the Scarab, one of the fun rescue boats, out on a cruise to impress his friends. The children go to a deserted island, get lost, and run out of fuel. One of them gets hurt. Then they are all taken hostage by an evil man hiding out on the island. The kids manage to escape, and Mitch shows up to rescue them after spotting the Scarab on high-tech radar equipment.

One short, sharp, blast of my whistle rings through the air. "No running on the pool deck!" I shout over the Marco Polo game to my right and the laughing and splashing to my left. A minute later I hear the ring of another guard's whistle from across the pool. "No diving here! The water is too shallow!" he yells as the small girl dives from the deck anyway. No, we are not the whistle-happy freaks that some perceive us to be, yelling at every opportunity. Rather we are trying to prevent potential harm to swimmers by eliminating anything that could jeopardize their safety. Unlike the *Baywatch* guards, we put a stronger emphasis on "watching and trying to spot our victims before they're in trouble" (Fleishman 5).

Young bikini-clad sunbathers eye the hot lifeguard as he runs along the edge of the water. The female lifeguards, their hair bouncing in the breeze and their makeup perfectly applied, run into the waves to make a rescue. The rescue boat speeds away from a burning steamer just as BAYWATCH flashes across the screen.

The sun beats down relentlessly. I can already feel the sun turning my shoulders a pale shade of pink in spite of the thick layer of SPF 45 sun block I applied only an hour before. I am uncomfortable and beginning to sweat. Who said this job is supposed to be glamorous? This is not what guarding is about at all. There aren't two thousand admiring fans wearing thong bikinis lying on the beach, and there aren't any rescue boats or radar equipment. On the seven dollars we make an hour, we can't afford to look like Pamela Lee.

❖   ❖   ❖

There are many myths about lifeguarding. Some people believe lifeguards have a cushy job that lets them hang out at the beach, socialize, and get a fabulous tan. Others simply view guards as sex symbols who strut their stuff all day in a cute suit. Few, however, recognize the true importance of a guard. There is so much more to guarding than simply "sitting atop elevated chairs, [and] watching winter-white skin turn bronze" (Thompson 3). It is true that often we don't seem to be doing a whole heck of a lot, but ask any lifeguard and he or she will tell you it is "hard work, real hard work" (Recktenwald 3).

Drownings are not very common today, but that doesn't make them any less important or serious. Lives are on the line. During the summer of 1995 one special group of lifeguards proved how important their job really is. On August 13 of that year, the New Jersey Shore Seaside Heights Beach Patrol had a really terrible day. There were storms at sea, but it was hot and people were looking for a way to get a little relief from the heat. They were not prepared for the perils that awaited them in the water. The twenty-four-member patrol pulled well over a hundred and fifty swimmers from the water that day alone, but even their tremendous efforts could not save the ten who drowned that summer, most during the hours when guards were not on duty (Sharkey 1).

Even when there isn't a rescue to be made, drama unfolds everywhere there is water. It is there in "the day-to-day tension" as lifeguards watch in anticipation of what will happen next (Fleishman 5). There is an enormous amount of responsibility on the shoulders of the guards. They are entrusted with protecting your life while you swim, and they take their job seriously.

Baywatch is starting a new program, the Search and Rescue Team. Working with local firefighters, lifeguards will find and rescue victims from very dangerous situations. All the candidates go through a brief training period, parading around in their ever-cute swimsuits the whole time. Guards and firefighters are chosen to join the special unit just as a call comes in. There has been an explosion in a factory and two men are trapped inside. The team rushes into action: walls are drilled through, scuba equipment appears, and rescuers are hoisted down into the middle of massive debris. Neely, one of the guards chosen for the team, finds the first victim while another guard, Cody, locates the second. Neely lifts a heavy beam from on top of the man's body and brings him to safety. Cody hauls his unconscious victim out of the water that has flooded the room. He uses CPR to keep him alive and brings him to safety as well. It's a good thing they had so much training in those few days!

In order to become a guard "candidates must pass a grueling swimming test as well as complete first-aid and cardiopulmonary resuscitation training" (Recktenwald 3). To become certified, lifeguards must go through a six-week class, run by the Red Cross, that prepares them for the situations they could face. Guards are trained through a series of videos, practice drills with classmates, written exams, and skill exams. By the end of the class the ABCs (airway, breathing, and circulation) have become so rote they can say them in their sleep. In fact, that is the intention. When a real emergency arises all of one's emotions are caught up in what is happening. Being so familiar with the skills gives the rescuer the assurance to do what is needed as second nature. Although we all hope these skills will never have to be practiced, they are imperative to know. Certain jobs may require that additional criteria be met. For instance, at the Cape Cod National Seashore lifeguards must pass a "Surf Rescue School" exam: "a half-mile run on the sand and a 500-yard ocean swim in under 20 minutes" (Zernike 13).

❖   ❖   ❖

Even after the long day of guarding, Baywatch's hottest couple get to-gether for a romantic dinner. Logan has prepared a special meal for Caroline. He takes her down to the beach and builds a small fire in the sand as she lays the blanket down. After dinner he professes his undying love for her, completely confident that she will not mind waiting for him until he can marry a rich older blonde woman, get his green card, and then divorce her.

It has been a long, hot day at the pool I am glad it is finally over. The only time I've been in the water was when I took a dip during my short break. Walking out of the pool, I see a guard I haven't seen all day. We must have been working on opposite sides. I pack up my bag and pull my shirt on over my head. I didn't make any saves today. No assists. I didn't get to be a hero, but all my swimmers were safe. It was a great day.

Works Cited

Fleishman, Sandra. "Life vs. 'Baywatch': On the Job, TV Cast and Real Crews are Oceans Apart." *Washington Post,* 29 July 1996, sec. D, p. 5.

Recktenwald, William. "Font of Lifeguards Found in CHI." *Chicago Tribune,* 6 August 1996, sec. 2C, p. 3.

Sharkey, Joe. "The End of a Perilous Season in the Surf." *New York Times,* 3 September 1995, NJ sec., p. 1.

Thompson, Neal. "It's Wall Street Over 'Baywatch' in Search for Summer Work." *Christian-Science Monitor,* 30 July 1996, p. 3.

Zernike, Kate. "The Unchanging of the Guard." *Boston Globe,* 8 July 1996, p. 13.

Thoughts on Augustine's God

Ari Shapiro

In his *Confessions*, Augustine describes how he eventually becomes an extremely pious person. He also questions the nature of God, God's role in the universe, and the special relationship God and human beings share. In writing these *Confessions*, Augustine is not questioning his faith but rather using his faith as a basis for articulating his questions. Nor does Augustine answer many of these questions; instead he allows readers to frame their own response in the context of their own perspective. Readers must probe their own religious beliefs as they grow to understand Augustine's theological and moral viewpoint. The *Confessions* thus serves both as a means for Augustine to convey his youthful experiences, his lustful adolescence, and the joy of his eventual conversion and as a forum in which to pose theological questions that remain unanswered.

In the third section of Book 1, Augustine expresses his desire to understand whether heaven and earth contain God or whether God fills them completely, making it impossible for them to contain Him. He also questions whether God fills larger entities with more of Himself than smaller entities. Augustine concerns himself with the three-dimensional realm of God, curious about what boundaries define Him if He is finite and what part of our world He fills if He is infinite. Wrestling with Augustine's questions myself, I draw upon my ideas regarding God as influenced by His depiction in the Old Testament and the parental and secular instruction I have received. I feel that if God is truly omnipotent and omnipresent, He is not contained by a world defined by human beings. Although perhaps not palpably present in all areas of the universe, His awareness encompasses infinite space. I also believe an all-powerful God is not confined to existing in a single temporal frame of reference as human beings are. Although humans are restricted to a linear existence, God is aware of the past, present, and future simultaneously. I therefore do not restrict God to a three-dimensional existence, but rather consider the potential for His omnipotent and infinite awareness in four dimensions.

In the sixth section of Book 10, Augustine examines the manifestation of God and concludes that God is His *creations* and that He is reflected in the life of the earth. This opinion resonates strongly for me, because the intricate beauty of life, in both the macroscopic and microscopic realms, strikes me constantly. I have always been in awe of the beauty that surrounds us. The cyclical patterns of the seasons, the playful and aggressive interactions between organisms, the crisp aromas of the earth, and the delicate textures of nature are a few examples of natural phenomena that inspire me. I discovered the scientific basis for these phenomena in the classes and books to which I was later exposed. I am intrigued that a natural occurrence is accompanied by an exquisitely beautiful macroscopic result. (Leaves, for example, lose their chlorophyll in the fall, leaving other red and orange pigments called the carotenoids behind. This causes the breathtaking autumnal reds, oranges, and yellows that so delight us.) I feel that a higher being of some kind has allowed for the integration of these natural processes with such beautiful sensory demonstrations.

In advanced biology classes, I have been able to probe more deeply into the molecular foundation of life, examining biochemical pathways, the molecular nature of heredity, and chemical reactions vital to the functioning of a cell. As a result I have an even deeper awe of our surroundings. The molecular basis for protein synthesis, for example, is amazing in its intricacy, simplicity, and functionality. This mechanism is conserved across all species, revealing its consistency despite organismal and environmental differences. I find these molecular components of life exciting because the diversity on earth emerges from the same molecular processes. The consistency and efficiency again lead me to hypothesize some type of divine influence that has allowed life to develop in such a manner.

This train of thought also raises questions relating to the origin of life within an organism. Some scientists refute the existence of God by claiming that evolution favored simple solutions to tasks necessary to life. What, then, endows a creature with life and what causes that life to dissipate into death? What provides a human being with consciousness and self-awareness? Molecular interactions and evolution are less-than-compelling explanations. It is the synergistic component of life that I feel suggests most strongly the presence of God. It is impossible to determine precisely what living organisms contain that endow them with the life inanimate objects do not possess. Science is capable of explaining enzymatic interactions and predator-prey relationships, but the element that breathes life into living organisms remains a mystery.

I am fascinated with the biological sciences' inability to answer theological questions dealing with the influence of God on the earth and life. That inability allows me to take a philosophical approach to my increasing scientific knowledge and awareness. I feel it is essential that a student studying the sciences never forget the moral and ethical questions to which science has not yet found, and may never find, the solutions. Augustine's *Confessions* encourages such reflection as Augustine discloses his theological and moral realizations. Augustine's questions serve as a catalyst for his further reflections on God and as a means of stimulating readers to confront their own conceptions of the nature of God and the role of God in life.

Is it Too Much Pressure?

Colleen Wenke

You hear the clock ticking in your head, and your teacher keeps erasing, in ten-minute decrements, the time you have left to complete the test. You do not remember anything from the last month of class. You probably should have studied more, watched less television, and spent less time on the phone. All the "should haves" are not important now. You need to finish the test and get out of here. The thought of a big fat F and a "See me" on the top of your midterm scares you. You remember the small piece of paper you have hidden in your pocket just in case. For a fleeting moment you think about what will happen if you are caught; then you slip the paper from your pocket onto the desktop. You transfer all the required information onto the test in time. You smile in anticipation of the A you are going to get. You think of how easy it was to cheat. All that matters is getting the grade.

Cheating is taking work done by somebody else, be it a friend or someone you do not know, and writing your name on it and saying it is your work. Anytime I walked through my high school cafeteria or the hallways, I saw people cheating. It came in many forms, from copying homework to giving out copies of the exam. Students even wrote the answers to a scantron exam down the sides of number-2 pencils and gave the pencils to their friends. My history teacher freshman year had a name for these students: "cafeteria scholars." These were the students who pulled nineties by knowing what the test questions were before they got to the classroom. Their friends who had taken the exam earlier in the day would tell them the questions and answers during lunch. The teachers knew that these things went on, yet nobody seemed to do anything about them. I thought this was the way school went. The people who were cheating were doing the best in all of my classes. I would study for hours and still pull Bs. They would pull As.

I remember conversations over the dinner table with my parents
on the subject of cheating. My parents were disgusted at the apathetic views
my brothers and I held. We really didn't think it was a big deal to copy
homework. I thought everyone cheated, probably even my parents and
teachers when they were my age. But my parents swore that they had never
cheated. Did I believe them? Not really. I thought that they were giving us
the "it was so much better when we were growing up" speech.

I soon learned differently. In the article "When the Ends Justify the
Means," written by Robin Stansbury, a reporter for the Connecticut newspaper *The Courant*, I found that my parents were telling the truth. Stansbury
reports that "cheating in school has probably been around since the first
exam was given." But he goes on to say, "State and national statistics show
cheating among high school students has risen dramatically during the
past fifty years" (2). Reading this upset me and made me think about what
had caused this increase. I hoped this was not a reflection of moral decline
in the people who would soon be running my country. I blamed our school
system for not instilling the proper values in its students. I figured that the
dramatic change in the role of the family over the past generation, from
two-parent homes with a working father and a mother who stayed at home
and watched her children to families which have only a single parent or in
which both parents work outside the home, meant schools needed to include moral standards in the curriculum. I believed schools were not
fulfilling their role and therefore were producing students who do not know
the difference between right and wrong.

An article written by Robert L. Maginnis, a policy analyst in the
Cultural Studies Project at the Family Research Council, indicates my hy-
pothesis had some truth to it. Maginnis states that "the erosion of values is
traceable largely to changes in institutions which have traditionally been
responsible for imparting them to our youth." He defines "these key institutions [to] include family, school, church, media and government" (1). I
agree with Maginnis, but I can't accept these factors as the only sources in
the increase of cheating in the classroom. The facts seem contradictory. If
my parent's generation had such high morals and wouldn't cheat, wouldn't
they teach their children the same? My parents had taught me that cheating was wrong, yet I seemed to accept it.

There is a new "class" of cheaters today. In the past, as one would
expect, the students who cheated were the ones who could not pass or did
not do the work. They were the lazy students. But today the majority of the
students who admit to cheating are college-bound overachievers. The students who are trying to juggle too many activities are resorting to

compromising their integrity for a good grade. There is too much competition between students, which leads to increased pressure to do well. Cheating becomes a way to get the edge over the other students in the class. In addition, penalties for getting caught are mild. If you were caught cheating at my high school, you received a zero for the test. Your parents were not called, and you were not suspended. True, a zero would hurt your grade severely if all grades for each quarter counted. But there was a loophole in the system: each quarter the lowest grade was dropped. If the zero grade was dropped, it made no difference; the average was not affected. Students who cheated on all the tests but only got caught once still received good grades.

A main difference between school today and school when my parents were enrolled is that we are now very goal-oriented and will compromise our values to achieve these goals. Stansbury sees this compromise of values and reports in his article that "cheating is a daily occurrence in high school. . . . What this says is that many of our students today do not have much internal integrity." Stansbury argues that students "want a goal, and how to get the goal is somewhat irrelevant" (3). Today there is more pressure placed on students to do well. They are expected to receive good grades, play a sport, and volunteer if they are to be looked at by a good college. With a B tainting your transcript, a college might not look at you. This new pressure is what is causing the increase in cheating. Maginnis agrees with Stansbury and goes further, reporting, "A national survey found a shift in motivation away from altruism and toward concern with making money and getting power and status." Like Stansbury, Maginnis says "students are finding it easier to rationalize lying or cheating in pursuit of their goals" (2). And what goals are these students pursuing? They want the best grades so that they can get into the best schools and get the highest-paying jobs. Starting in the classroom, we are sending the message that it is acceptable to cheat as long as you do not get caught and you do the best.

Dean Morton, a broadcaster for *Good Morning America*, reported that according to a national survey conducted in 1997 by *Who's Who in American High School Students*, as many as 98 percent of students who participated in the survey admitted to cheating. The segment of the show was even entitled "Guess What? Cheaters Do Prosper." Like Stansbury and Maginnis, this survey also concluded that it is now the common belief among students that cheaters are getting ahead in life. Stansbury interviewed several high school students in his article and discovered that many of them feel cheaters do get ahead in the classroom: "In high school, the cheaters always win. They don't get caught and they are the ones getting

100 on the exams when the noncheaters are getting 80s and 90s. Cheaters do win" (5). We are sending a message to our youth that it is acceptable to cheat as long as you don't get caught and you are getting As. In this kind of society, morals take a back seat to how much you earn and how prosperous you are.

Students who would not usually cheat get sucked into believing it is the only way to get ahead in school: if the cheaters are doing better than they are and not getting caught, then they better try it. Stansbury proposes that there is such an enormous increase in cheating because more students are joining in: "They see others cheating and they think they are being unfairly disadvantaged." He adds that the "only way many of them feel they can keep in the game, to get into the right schools, is to cheat" (6). In high school I always felt at a disadvantage, because everybody else was cheating and doing better than I was, even if only by a few points. My friends felt the same way, that copying work or cheating was the only way to keep up with the rest of the class. It frustrated me, because the cheaters were not earning their grades. But there were plenty of times when I was in a jam and copied homework from friends. Thinking about this now, I wonder what allowed me to push aside my conviction that cheating was wrong. I wasn't bringing in cheat sheets and didn't know the questions to tests before I got there, but I was cheating nonetheless.

How should we respond to the huge increase in cheating over the past generation? We need to step back and look at the broader picture. We are creating a society in which people feel it is acceptable to cheat. This attitude will not stop in the classroom, but will carry on into the business world. Those who are cheating are the ones getting the grades and getting into the best schools. They are the "smart" ones. They in turn are the ones who will be running our country. They will become the heads of businesses and presidents of big corporations. Are these the people we want to have the power? In all likelihood they will not stop cheating once they get to the top. They become the people we idolize and aspire to be like. Because they are powerful, we consider them clever, highly respectable people. I do not hold any respect for a dishonest cheater. The phrase "honest businessman" will truly be an oxymoron. I am scared to think of the consequences of having cheaters rule our country. Is our society teaching that this is the only way to get ahead in life? Does obtaining status and power make you good? Schools are drifting away from emphasizing learning and are emphasizing the grade instead. When the thirst for knowledge is replenished in a student's mind, the desire for the grade without the work will dissolve. Only then will cheating decline.

Works Cited

Maginnis, Robert L. *Cheating Scandal Points to Moral Decline*, 1–4. Family Research Council, April, 1994. Available on-line at: http:/lwww.abic.ore/frc/perspeceivelpv94dled.html(AltaVista)

Stansbury, Robin. "Cheating in Connecticut's Classrooms: When the Ends Justify the Means." *The [Hartford] Courant*, March 2, 1997, 1, 6. Available on-line at: ht~p://news.courant.com/speciaUcheating/daYl.h~

Special Report Survey (1997) conducted by *Who's Who in American High School Students*. Quoted on ABC's *Good Morning America*, April 16, 1997.

Seventeen Mixed Messages

Sarah Freeman

❦

"Staying cool has never been this easy!" Easy as what? you may ask. *Seventeen* magazine and others of its type are ready and waiting to fill "the modern teenage girl" in on what she needs to do to be "cool." Popularity is only a subscription away. But shouldn't the magazines young girls read be teaching them to have confidence in themselves, to aim for whatever goals they want, to realize their individuality?

Unfortunately, every step that is taken toward developing the self-esteem of a teenage girl seems to be wiped out with two steps backward when she reads an issue of *Seventeen*. Articles such as "The Reluctant Romeo," "The Latest Gotta-Have-It Beauty Booty," and "Trend-O-Rama" do not do the best job of fostering a sense of self-worth in teenage girls. I had a subscription to the magazine all through high school, but only when I look through a copy now do I realize just how wrong are the messages *Seventeen* sends.

At first glance, the May 1998 issue of *Seventeen* appears innocent enough; Leonardo DiCaprio, the latest teen heartthrob, adorns the cover. When you glance through the index, though, you realize how trivial the matters discussed are. Under fashion is "Nine Beauty Disasters and How to Fix Them." Why does the magazine feel the need to call them disasters? It's as if a girl's life is expected to end if she finds herself on this list. When I read through the article, I was surprised to find that many of the items on the list are actually encouraged in other parts of the magazine. For example, one of the "disasters" is tanning, something I think everyone these days will agree is bad for a person's health. But turn a few pages and there is a Hawaiian Tropics ad "for extreme tanners only!" Some girls may find themselves very confused.

The article that surprised me the most told girls what swimsuits they should wear this season to hide their figure flaws. Now, I've heard all the claims that the media is not affecting America's girls, that the huge number of girls with eating disorders is in no way related to what they see and read on television or in magazines. The thing is, I cannot get myself to overlook the blatant messages that are shown every day in the media. The idea that your figure is something you should be embarrassed by is not one we should be planting in developing minds. Women come in many different shapes and sizes. At one time, a variety of body shapes were admired in a woman, but somewhere along the way the "perfect" figure became almost sickly looking. I can't see why a magazine aimed at all "modern" teenage girls would choose to portray only one body type as acceptable. And not only does it focus on only one body type, it tells girls with any other body type how to hide it. One of the captions in the swimsuit article states, "Way-below-your-button boy bottoms draw attention to your tummy while hiding hips and covering your butt." Should a fifteen-year-old really feel she needs to hide her hips? Most of the girls who read *Seventeen* haven't even developed hips yet. (I should also note that all the suits, regardless of what "flaw" the article claims they can fix, are pictured on models who do not have the figure problem.)

Each issue of *Seventeen* contains numerous articles informing readers of the new "must have" items for every season. The items chosen for May include blue rhinestone sunglasses, color-crazy cowgirl hats, and bamboo thongs. If *Seventeen* is really directed toward all "modern" girls, it should be aware that not all teenage girls can afford to buy a new wardrobe with matching accessories every time the weather changes; it should shift its emphasis away from material things. Why is it you rarely find articles informing girls how they can make the most of what they have, both inside and out? The focus of the magazine seems always to be on the trivial and superficial aspects of life. One page of the May issue is devoted to Cameron Diaz's "true passion" in life. You may be surprised to learn that it is not her work or her family. According to *Seventeen* it is the "perpetual pursuit of the perfect purse."

One of the more serious articles I came across informs girls how to deal with competition when it comes to guys. Not just any competition, mind you, but competition from your mother. The caption at the top of the page reads: "She gave birth to you, changed your diapers, taught you how to use scissors—so what's up with her sudden flirting with your boyfriend and borrowing your clothes?" The last I heard this is not one of the most pressing issues facing girls today. It's bad enough magazines like this put so much emphasis on relationships at this age, let alone a mother's involvement in them.

The magazine would also have a girl believe she is not normal if she does not have a boyfriend at age fourteen. In a question/answer section, a reader writes in asking, "I'm thirteen and I feel as if boys don't even notice me.... Do you think that [my] glasses and books are the reason guys ignore me?" What answer does the columnist give? Not the one you might expect. "You should look into getting contact lenses. They might make you feel more comfortable." The response lacks any form of encouragement to disregard what others think and trust in oneself. Although many girls of this age do choose to date, more attention needs to be given to the reality that it is perfectly normal to choose not to as well. A sense of balance seems to be lacking here.

And it's not just the content of the magazine that is sending young girls the wrong message. The advertisements are as much to blame as the articles. Cosmetics advertisements are the most prevalent. I can remember, in seventh grade, asking my mother if I could go get my colors done so I would know what makeup I should wear to look good. To tell you the truth, I really had no desire to wear makeup, but magazines like *Seventeen* led me to believe it was the thing to do. (A question: if cosmetics brands claim to make their users appear youthful, why do they advertise to youth?)

One ad that truly puzzled me posed the question, "What are you without emotion?" Turning to the next page, I found out that the cosmetics manufacturer Bonne Bell is encouraging readers to "be emotional . . . be yourself." How? By buying their new line of fragrances, Bottled Emotion. Among the fragrances being presented were Hopeful, Playful, Flirty, and Pretty. Are these the emotions that should be presented to girls as important? And how is a girl being encouraged to be herself if she needs to buy a certain product to do so?

If I sound preachy, I apologize. But I am concerned for the young women of future generations. All the talk that goes on these days about giving girls more positive images to look toward as examples is simply not enough. Too many young women today are being raised to think that their most important job is to look good. We need to counteract this message with one that encourages girls to reach for whatever they want. I believe that women have come a long way in our society, but we cannot make the mistake of thinking it is far enough. As long as magazines like *Seventeen* are instilling the wrong ideals in their readers, much still needs to be done.

Part Four

Meditation

Neighborhood

Elizabeth Murphy

❦

When I think of my childhood summers I see a band of sun-bleached children, dehydrated from long days of forays. Scrapes mark their knees and mud cakes their sneakers. I see children scheming and cheating. I see children calling rocks mountains and pools oceans. We knew every corner of the woods behind our houses, and we knew the best bumps to ride our bikes over on our street. We were a neighborhood, and though our friendships were determined more by geography than anything else, we were the best of friends.

We would rouse each other at the crack of dawn. "Andrew," I'd call to my best friend, "let's go!" I don't know where we had to go, but everything we did held such purpose. Each day was wondrous, and each night that brought that day to an end was sad.

I thought they would last forever, the simple relationships, the care-free days, but nothing lasts for long.

Last summer I felt for the first time the silence that had claimed my neighborhood. When I was young our neighborhood was never quiet; it was a series of cries: battle cries against the imaginary monsters we were running from, our names called by our mothers at different pitches and speeds (usually to remind us to perform some life function that had slipped our mind, like, eating, bathing, or sleeping). I can still hear my mother: "Eeeelizaaabeeth, Elizzzzzzzabeth, Elizabeth!" When I think of that now, it seems so primal. Life then was simple and good. These days I could never run through my neighborhood screaming, and my mother would never resort to hollering my name from a window when she could not find me.

Summer cries no longer course through my neighborhood. There are no children running wildly through the woods forging new paths and trails. An occasional child, decked in protective gear from head to toe, rollerblades down the street. The rest of the neighborhood children spend their days in summer camps or in front of video games, a pastime my generation marginally, but thankfully, missed.

What happened? Where are all the kids, and when did I stop being one? What exact summer was it, and how did I not feel the change? What I have are memories . . .

When I went to first grade my best friend, Andrew, was devastated. He was a year younger than I, and this made him a kindergartner, and somewhat of a lesser life form to me. On my first day he walked me to the bus stop; I can still remember him waving, " Bye, Bossy." True, a minor speech impediment prevented him from being able to say Bethy, but Bossy was an appropriate nickname for me at the time. When I returned home that day, Andrew was there waiting for me, sitting where I had left him. He had waited for me all day. He had a pail and a shovel and asked me to go shovel some sidewalk sand with him. I declined. This newly minted first grader found shoveling sand somewhat juvenile.

"Andrew," I explained, " first graders have more important things to do than shovel sand." It breaks my heart to this day to think how I left him there, dejected, hurt.

I guess the beginning of school always brought an end to our close neighborly ties, but the slightest bit of warm weather would bring us all together again. It was almost instinctive. When school ended in late spring, it felt unnatural to play with school friends. School friends didn't know where the secret shortcuts in the neighborhood were, and they didn't know where thickets of grapes and blackberries lay hidden in a neighbor's yard. As our neighborhood friendships became obsolete in the fall, so did our school friendships wane in the summer. The neighborhood kids were all great friends again until Labor Day weekend, and then we started saying our good-byes. The ritual of back-to-school shopping and picking out new lunch boxes meant it was time once again to put away our summer clothes and summer friends.

I guess I do remember the first time I felt too old to be one of the neighborhood kids. The stress of being a fifth grader had set in, heavily. I had a book report due, and a ton of long-division problems. I heard laughter down on the street. I looked out my window and saw some boys in my neighborhood riding their bikes. I was jealous; they seemed so free. They didn't know that their carefree fourth-grade days were numbered and soon they would have as many deadlines and obligations as I had. At that moment I felt old, mature.

The summer that followed this little revelation was the first one during which I really missed my school friends. We had started to forge more mature relationships during the year, ones that were not built on playing games but on our thoughts, discussions, and experiences. I left the neighborhood behind that summer. The children younger than I couldn't understand why I didn't want to play or why I went to other friends' houses on other streets. But they would find out. One by one they would each graduate to my status.

Why is it that year by year the echoing cries are fewer, the children outside more scarce? There is always another generation, isn't there? There is always another gaggle of girls and boys to whom the sacred secrets of a neighborhood are passed down through some subliminal ritual. But not in my neighborhood. We were the last generation who valued fighting the dragons and monsters hiding in trees and rocks rather than ones created by a computer. Swords made of sticks and brambles have been replaced by the control panels for Sega or Nintendo entertainment systems. Our breed is extinct, existing only in our memories.

A lot of the kids I spent those magical summers with are gone; they have either moved away or gone to college, like me. They return every so often and say, "Look, that's where we used to hide from our mothers when they called us to bed," or "That's where that mean dog lived who chased us all the time." But no one's hiding now. No one is running from any dogs. Everyone is inside.

Banana

Aliza Kimhachandra

So you call me a banana. Well, maybe I am one, what's it to you anyway? I didn't ask to be born one, but I was, and you will just have to accept me for what I am. A banana is a wonderful fruit.

My parents come from Thailand, a beautiful tropical country in Southeast Asia. I was born in America, but I am still Thai at heart. Actually, my yellow skin has been something of an asset. Attached to my appearance is a long string of stereotypes: Asian girls are quiet and obedient; they all play the piano; they are smart little robots that do everything right; they are like computers, studying all the time and storing information. There is not much creativity in these robots, but they can make the grade and that's what's important. Throughout primary and most of secondary school it was very easy for me to fall into these stereotypes. All those things that parents, teachers, and administrators like. I was a very quiet student. The only time I spoke was when I was sure what I was about to say was not stupid. This was usually a correct answer to some math problem, which led everyone to believe I was a whiz. I never disrupted class. I always did what I was told. I played the piano. I was the stereotypical Asian kid.

To add to my "yellowness," after years of being ignorant about my Asian heritage, I became a self-made expert on Thai culture. In high school, people would come to me and say, "You were born and raised in America, how come you're so Thai? How do you know so much about Thailand? And how come you can still speak Thai?" Well, it's inevitable. When most of your life you've seen people with round light eyes, light skin, and light hair, characteristics you don't have, and then you take a trip and begin to see people with slanted dark eyes, dark hair, and a tan complexion, characteristics you do have, you have to question yourself. "Hey, self, why do you look like those people when you speak and act like these people?" This question swallowed me up and I had to find the answer. In my search, I ended up teaching myself to speak and read Thai and learning all I could about Thai traditions and customs. It's really interesting how much ethnicity affects a person's way of thinking. It's like a conscience. For example, if you ask an Asian what she needs to eat to become full, she would most likely respond by saying, "Rice." But if you ask an Irish person the same question, wouldn't that person say, "Potatoes"? Anyway, you understand what I mean.

My white part, under the yellow skin, is my American side. It's a funny thing. I was kind of living a double life all through school. While in school, it was more advantageous to act Asian, so that's what I did. Outside school, in society, it was more advantageous to act American. Outgoing and friendly, talkative, I became all these outside the classroom. Friends from school have always found it strange that my personality changes so much depending on whether I am inside or outside class. It's just a matter of fitting in and assessing what kind of behavior is more advantageous in certain places. When I tell them this, they understand why I change, but it is still difficult for them to understand how I can be so American and also be so Thai. Well, everyone knows that America is made up of immigrants. In the area I live in now, there are many Americans of Italian descent. They have western features, for the most part they speak with an American accent, and their families have been in America for generations. They don't question whether they are American or not and neither do their peers and colleagues; of course they are American. But if we look closer at these families, they are still very Italian. They eat a lot of pasta, spend hours preparing meat sauce from an old family recipe, abide by the Catholic church. They are still very Italian, but are also very American.

After a long period of thinking and trying to understand who I am—am I really able to be both Thai and American? am I more Thai or more American?—I realized that I really am both. A unique mixture of East and West. So I began to act like both. I took the bad aspects of the cultures, like female inferiority, and threw them away; then I picked up their good characteristics and meshed them together to make . . . well, me. Now I can be smart, loud, obedient yet daring, all the good stuff that is associated with being Asian and being American. The next thing I need to do is to try and get others to understand this about me.

Most of those people who say I am *so* Asian are white Americans. On the other hand, those who say I am *so* American are Asian. If my analysis is correct, this stems from the very human tendency of a group of similar people to notice more readily the differences in people who are not so similar to themselves. To the typical white American, who sees "American" acts everyday and is immune to them, my Asian side is definitely different and they notice these differences. The same goes for the Asians. To them, I am very American because they notice the American things I do while they are immune to the Asian things. An example: If I bow to an elder in the Thai community, non-Thais will take more notice than Thais would. On the other hand, if I'm wearing a tank top and shorts, Thais will take more notice because for Thais dressing this way in public is improper. I think it's funny how neither group can accept me as both Asian *and* American. I guess it's just human nature to try to put things into specific categories. It's too bad, though, because it shows that people don't realize what America is— a wonderful nation enriched by the diversity of her people.

So I am a banana. Being a banana is not at all bad. There are many advantages to being one. It is a unique fruit that has its own characteristics, way of growth, and way of presenting itself to the world. It is a distinct member of the fruit family. It is sweet and satisfying. I love being a banana. And have you ever noticed that after peeling back its golden yellow skin, the ripe pulp of a banana is actually a shade of pale yellow? A harmonious mixture of yellow and white together in a sweet, wonderful fruit. It's a nice color, perfectly acceptable, but not many people notice it. Here's my final question: if I am a banana, unique, sweet, wonderful . . . what kind of fruit are you?

Silent Cries

Sayat Ozcan

The Armenian villagers march, one in front of the other, down the dusty road, under the watchful eye of the Turkish soldiers. They pass house after house, each deserted. Passing one tiny shack, they don't realize there is a scared little Armenian girl inside. Ani huddles underneath her bed, whimpering and shaking. She is struck with fear as she listens to the stomping of boots and cries of terror that come from outside. She squeezes her eyes shut and tightens her grip on her doll. She remembers how they took away her mother, her two little brothers, and her beautiful older sister. The soldier yelled at Ani's mother in Turkish, telling her to gather her things and come along. Then he put his large dirty hand around her sister's arm and dragged her out the door. Ani starts to cry, hard. She wonders if her family are dead, if she will ever see them again. She wonders if the Turks will find her and take her away, and whether she will survive. She wonders if anybody can hear her crying.

Eighty-two years later and thousands of miles away, I sit in a class-room at Boston College, thinking. It's Friday. I am in theology class and am supposed to be joining in a discussion of an article we have read about the Jewish Holocaust. The article hit me hard. I have to step back from what is being said. I feel like the guy in the movies who starts to doze off while people around him are still talking, their words turning into mumbling or background noise. I think about one of the most tragic events in Armenian history—the Armenian Genocide. It is not a topic new to my thoughts. Lately, however, I have come to see it from, or through, another perspective. Lately my interest in the topic has grown stronger. I have become hungrier for information than ever before. My way of thinking about the topic has changed from when I first heard about it as a seven-year-old. To understand how my feelings have changed, it is crucial to know a little bit about this tragic event in Armenian history.

Toward the end of the nineteenth century, as the Ottoman Empire was beginning to crumble, the Turks began looking for a scapegoat. The Armenians became their target, because they were a Christian people living in the empire who had become very successful businessman, artisans, and intellectuals. The Turks blamed the Armenians for the decline of the empire and believed the Armenians were conspiring against it. Their reasoning, which was similar to Hitler's ideas about the Jews, led to a plan of destruction. As the nineteenth century came to a close, hundreds of thousands of Armenian men, women, and children were killed in what is now central and eastern Turkey. These mass murders continued into the next century: the Turkish government carried out the largest of these massacres, known as the Armenian Genocide, during the years 1915 to 1923. One and a half million Armenians were driven from their homes and forced out into the Syrian deserts, where they were starved, slaughtered, and left to die. Although most of the world knew what was going on, nobody did anything to stop it, and the tragedy was largely ignored in the years that followed. Not until the latter part of this century have governments publicly recognized the Armenian Genocide. The Turkish government still denies its attempt to systematically murder a people, claiming that the one and a half million deaths were mere casualties of civil war. However, many Armenians were able to escape to the United States, the Middle East, Russia, Canada, and South America. Some, like my family, survived even though they remained in Turkey. These survivors have another story.

I sit across from my grandmother at the kitchen table. Her silence tells me she is trying hard to retrieve from her memory the answers to my questions. I glance at my mom, who also waits while her mother pieces together all the names and stories in her mind. The silence continues. My grandmother looks out the window. Finally she looks at me, takes a deep breath, and begins telling me about her family.

Her mother, Zabel, was born and raised in Istanbul. Zabel and her parents were fortunate enough not to be directly affected by the Genocide. However, my grandmother's father, Shnork, experienced the Genocide firsthand. At age sixteen, during World War I, he was forced into the Turkish army. When the Turks pulled out of the war, he was released and came home only to find that his entire family, save for a brother, had been murdered.

My grandmother stops. We are silent as we reflect on what she has just told us. I break the silence by asking about my grandfather's, her husband's, family. My grandfather, Arsen, was born in Tokat. His mother,

Mariam, also of Tokat, watched her entire family being taken away to be slaughtered. She herself, at the age of ten, was slashed and left for dead. As she lay there, at night, she could hear the moans of the dying, and she sometimes drank from the pools of blood surrounding her, in an attempt to stay alive. Mariam's husband, Arout, was a young man when the Genocide first began. He fled to the mountains surrounding Tokat and joined local rebel forces, which waged attacks on Turkish soldiers. He returned to his village after some time and found that his entire family had been massacred. He eventually married Mariam, whose family had suffered the same fate.

All is silent once again. My father, who has just gotten home from work, enters the kitchen. I summarize what we have been discussing. Then I ask him the same questions I asked my grandmother half an hour before. He thinks for a few seconds, then begins telling me about his family.

His mother's mother, Gulum, was born and raised in Istanbul and did not experience the Genocide firsthand. Her husband, Garabed, was not as fortunate. Born and raised in Bilecik, he was drafted into the Turkish army during World War I. After the war, he returned home and found that his wife and child had been massacred. He moved to Istanbul some time later, where he met my great-grandmother and started another family. My paternal grandfather's family suffered a similar fate. My great-great-grandfather left his family in the care of friends and relatives and moved to the mountains around Kayseri when the massacres first began, toward the end of the nineteenth century. He was a rebel soldier, whom the Turks called Khacho the Devil, because he was responsible for so many of their deaths.

I thank both my father and grandmother for sharing some family history. I am touched by the amazing stories of suffering and courage. I had never thought about the Genocide in such personal terms. I never thought about how it affected my own family. Until the last couple of years, the Genocide had been a sad story we learned about in Armenian school.

I always knew that my people had experienced a great tragedy at the hands of the Turks. I knew they had been killed and their land had been taken away. It never really evoked anything more than sadness in me. I thought about it mostly during a few weeks in April, particularly on April 24, the day Armenians remember the Armenian Genocide. I never felt the urge to tell people about it. I never thought about how much publicity it got or didn't get. Everyone I knew knew about the Genocide. My world did not extend past the Armenian community. Then I grew up.

I am back in theology class. My thinking about the Genocide has changed so much. Do I have anything against Jews or the fact that the Holocaust receives so much attention? No. If anything, I sympathize with Jews.

Am I jealous or angry that the Jewish Holocaust receives so much more attention than the Armenian Genocide? Yes. It is very painful to feel ignored or neglected. There are no museums in Washington, DC, no *Schindler's List*, and not too many books or articles written about the Armenian Genocide. With age, I have become more aware that the Armenian tragedy of 1915–1923 does not get the attention it deserves.

As my feelings toward the Genocide have changed, so have my feelings toward myself. The Armenian Genocide has shaped me as a person even though I did not experience it firsthand. I feel I have a responsibility to tell people about it. This is a responsibility all Armenians share: to never forget and make sure the world does not forget. I plan to share the story through writing and film. But everyone must choose his or her own way.

The sounds of the soldiers and the people marching fade away. Ani gets out from under the bed. She is still terrified, but now it's more of being alone than of death. She steps carefully out the door. The dirt road is empty. She stands in the middle of it, staring in the direction she thinks the people were marching, holding her doll by its arm. These people, like her family, are not coming back. A great sadness wells up in her heart, rises up through her throat, into her eyes, and down her pale cheeks. Ani walks slowly back into her house and sits on the bed. Her shoulders move up and down as she sobs. Her mama is gone. She is all alone. Can anyone hear her crying?

I do.

Part Five

Researched Human Interest

The Elusive Butterfly

Greg Tartaglia

✻

When I was a young boy, maybe about four years old, I tried to catch a butterfly. Actually, my mother helped me because I was always a little wary around insects, even pretty, colorful ones. We got a net and went out to the backyard to try to catch a monarch dining in Mom's flower bed. We never actually caught it—it would flutter out of the way as soon as the net came near it. It kept us busy for a while, until we finally gave up. Did everyone have this much trouble catching a simple, defenseless butterfly?

Later in life, I found out that some of the toughest men in America—major-league baseball batters—occasionally have the same problem. The only difference is they are equipped with a large wooden bat instead of a net and the fluttering object of their frustration is not a motley winged insect but the knuckleball. The knuckler is a near-impossible pitch to hit; former New York Yankee Bobby Murcer once said that trying to get a hit off knuckleballer Phil Niekro was "'like eating Jell-O with chopsticks" (Cohen). Big-leaguers approach it the way I approached butterflies as a child—with the utmost wariness.

Unlike "normal" pitches, where the spin determines how the ball moves, a knuckleball is thrown with very little spin. The pitcher grips the ball with the fingertips or fingernails (not with the knuckles, as the name would indicate), keeps the wrist stiff, and "pushes" it forward with almost no spin. Dennis Springer, a major-league knuckleball pitcher for the Tampa Bay Devil Rays, offers this advice relative to gripping and throwing a knuckler: "I grab the baseball like I am throwing a palm ball, then I raise my first two fingers [forefinger and middle finger], putting my fingertips into the ball. I try to keep a stiff wrist when throwing the ball so that when I release the ball, it comes out of my hand without spin" (Springer). It is also thrown very slowly, sometimes at almost half the speed of a fastball. "Thrown softly, the knuckleball is incapable of breaking anything. Except

101

maybe a batter's spirit" (Romano 23). Springer only throws it at about fifty to sixty-five miles per hour. In comparison, Nolan Ryan's fastball has been clocked at upwards of a hundred miles per hour.

The idea behind the knuckler is that if is thrown with little or no spin, it will be more susceptible to forces in the air on its way to the plate. The theory is, "as a knuckleball approaches home plate, it changes directions erratically in an apparently random manner" (Watts 960). Because of this random approach, a batter has difficulty predicting the ball's movement and making contact. Unfortunately, the pitcher and catcher often don't know what it's going to do either, leading to wild pitches and passed balls. According to Dennis Springer, "I have played catch with guys who throw good [knuckleballs] and I hate it. . . . Some guys really do have a good one that will move all over the place" (Springer).

But is this theory of a knuckleball's susceptibility to every gust of wind true? Scientists have studied a baseball's aerodynamics in order to figure out what makes a knuckler "dance" like it does. A baseball is not an entirely smooth sphere. Its stitches give it rough edges, and "scientists are focusing on the role of the baseball's stitches in creating turbulence in the airflow" (Flaste 364). Turbulence results when imperfections disrupt air flowing over a smooth surface. With pitches that spin, turbulence is not a factor, because the ball moves forward and spins fast enough to overcome the effects of turbulence on its way to home plate. However, if a baseball "is thrown with very little rotation, asymmetric stitch configurations can be generated that lead to large imbalances of forces and extraordinary excursions in trajectory" (Adair 29).

In other words, the stitches cause the air around a knuckleball to become turbulent, which in turn causes it to "bounce around" in the air. "At first the seams' aerodynamic influence might be pushing the ball outside, away from the plate; then, suddenly, a small shift in the seams might reverse the force, causing the ball to plunge back across the inside corner" (Flaste 366). The slight rotation of a knuckler causes that "small shift." So a knuckleball thrown without any spin is useless. Through wind-tunnel testing, scientists have found that "if the knuckleball is thrown in such a fashion that it has no spin at all, it can only curve laterally in one direction. . . . The single exception can occur in the remote possibility that the strings are initially positioned so that they disturb the point of boundary layer separation and bring about the oscillating wake phenomena (Watts 963).

This means that a nonspinning baseball will only move one way, unless the seams are perfectly aligned in a way that causes turbulence regardless of spin. In baseball speak, a nonspinning knuckler is said to behave like a "BP [batting practice] fastball," meaning it travels straight and is easy to hit. "Too much spin could prove disastrous, however, since the inertia of the ball would not allow a significant deflection" (963). A knuckleball that spins too much will also behave like a very slow fastball and most likely end up in the front row of the outfield bleachers. The most effective way to throw a knuckler is with just a slight rotation.

Different temperatures and air pressures also affect the way a knuckleball behaves. Springer observes, "I have always loved pitching in hot and humid weather. For some reason the ball just works better in those conditions. . . . I do not at all enjoy pitching in high altitudes such as Albuquerque or Denver. . . . There is no air in those high altitudes that will help the ball move" (Springer). In humid weather, there is more moisture in the air, which magnifies the effects of turbulence on a baseball. The exact opposite is true in high altitudes, where the thin air reduces turbulence. The lower the air pressure, the less effect the air has on the seams of the ball that disturb the airflow—if pitched in a vacuum, a knuckleball would move straight through the air.

One of the most important factors in considering how a knuckleball moves, though, is the pitcher. The knuckler is a tough pitch to get the hang of, and not everyone can throw it well. Only three knuckleball pitchers play in the major leagues today: Springer; Tom Candiotti, of the Athletics; and Tim Wakefield, of the Red Sox. Three is also the number of knuckleballers in the Baseball Hall of Fame: Phil Niekro, Hoyt Wilhelm, and Jesse Haines. This is a testament to how difficult it is to be a successful knuckleball pitcher. Springer commented, "I think just the fact that it took me almost nine years to make it to the big leagues proves that it is indeed a tough pitch to master. . . . It took me a long time to learn and I am still learning" (Springer). Because of its unpredictable nature, one can never throw it and expect consistent results. Springer also said, "It's just having the right feel" (Romano 3). His manager, the Devil Rays' Larry Rothschild, said, "You have to realize with a knuckleball pitcher that on bad days, they're going to be bad. On good days, they're able to beat anybody" (Romano). It's kind of a hit-or-miss situation. Even the best knuckleball pitchers have bad days.

Perhaps the knuckleball should be renamed the screwball—not just because you don't throw it off the knuckles, but because it's such an unusual pitch. Most people prefer to go to the ballpark to see a pitcher who can throw ninety-eight miles per hour or who baffles batters with a pinpoint curveball. The knuckler is somewhat of a novelty, and not just in baseball. "Like knuckleballers, researchers toiling at the crossroads of science and sports are few but dedicated. They are well aware that their work strikes some colleagues as mundane if quirky" (Flaste 367), which is how most people tend to feel about knuckleball pitchers. People often write them off. They think, "I could throw a pitch that slow." Perhaps they just don't understand all the factors that go into a knuckleball. For sure they never stood in the batter's box, flailed at, missed, and were completely embarrassed by the ever-elusive butterfly of pitches, the knuckler.

Works Cited

Adair, Robert K. *The Physics of Baseball,* p. 29. New York Harper Perennial, 1990.

Cohen, Eliot. "Baseball Lore: Knuckleballs." *Total Baseball.* 1996. Online. Available: http://www.totalbaseball.com/story~person/player/lore/knuckle.ht~

Romano, John. "Devil Rays Love Their Knucklehead." *Nando.net.* 1998. Online. Available: http://www.sportserver.corn/newsrc~m/sports/bbo/1998/rnlbltam/featl archive/032798/tam64861.html

Springer, Dennis. Pitcher, Tampa Bay Devil Rays. Personal interview, March 27, 1998.

Watts, Robert G. "Aerodynamics of a Knuckleball." *American Journal of Physics* 43 (November 1975): 960–63

Flaste, Richard, ed. "Why Does the Knuckleball Behave That Way?" In *The New York Times Book of Science Literacy,* 364–68. New York: Times Books, 1991.

The Best Defense

Jane Kim

What's the difference between a lawyer and a vampire?
A vampire only sucks blood at night.

Believe it or not, this joke and many others directed at the legal profession can be found on a free on-line service provided by the law offices of S. Wayne Rosenbaum. Apparently some lawyers have managed to keep a sense of humor amid today's lawyer-bashing craze. I must admit that I have often laughed at and believed people's negative judgments about the law profession. However, since my dorm arrangements this year found me living on the Newton campus, in the midst of the Boston College Law School (BCLS), I decided to find out the validity of these beliefs. One way to do so was to conduct an ethnography, that is, to "observe and describe the daily life, behaviors, and language of a group of people for long periods of time" (Chiseri- Strater 3).

I conducted my field research in the Stuart Law cafeteria. As I pushed open the heavy glass doors, I stopped a moment to catch my breath before venturing into the realm of the lawyers-to-be. Not-so-pleasing floor patterns of maroon and beige greeted my eyes, as did tiled pillars. I overheard two females comment on the "awful seventies" decor of the somewht enervating room, with its clash of colors, low ceiling, and ugly blue chairs reminiscent of a clinic. And although there are many windows in this room, the sunlight did a better job of blinding me than putting me in a relaxed or study-conducive mood. The nauseating odor of burritos, clam chowder, and other food permeated the air. I glanced over the drab, gray tables to see what the law students had chosen to eat for lunch, almost feeling sorry for them because of the gustatory indignities they had to suffer. Stuart food can be hard to digest , whether one has had a rough day in freshmen biology or been studying religiously for the bar.

Table Talk

On numerous occasions I had tiptoed through the Stuart halls wondering what exactly these law students talked about and whether they were indeed "superhuman." Now I took a seat at the far end of the cafeteria and listened in on conversations: perhaps the prospects and pressures of preparing for a legal career would come out naturally in this more laid-back atmosphere. Not surprisingly, much of what I overheard revolved around academia.

Two tables in front of me, two men, one in a plaid shirt , the other in a navy blue shirt, a baseball cap, and glasses, appeared to be in a heated discussion. Although I was unable to discern the exact content of their argument, I could tell that it was course-related. The plaid-clad man tapped the table to establish his point and strategically placed his index finger on his forehead in noticeable frustration, while his companion rebutted his arguments, paging through his binder for support.

Adjacent to these flustered men sat four women and one man. They were all casually dressed and had papers and books spread out across the table and BC coffee cups in hand. The male of the group was leaning so far back in his chair it seemed he might fall off. He commented on the clam chowder and the varieties of food that day. Then he went on to bemoan the length of the final. A woman in a light blue shirt confessed that it had taken her two hours to "BS" her way through it. (I suppose the art of making things up never dissipates, not even—especially?— in law school.) Another woman in the group sarcastically asked her companions if they could please explain the semester to her. The man then claimed that his professor had said "a lot of good stuff" but had "organized the class really strangely." As the group went on discussing "case studies," "federal rules versus state laws," and "statutes of limitations," I found myself not only confused but intrigued. They had obviously memorized many definitions and terms, most of them unfamiliar to me. Nevertheless, I could relate to their complaints and confusion about class material. Even their anxiety about having "so much work to do" is something that plagues freshmen. When their discussion/whining session ended, they collected their canvas-cased laptops, backpacks, and pocketbooks and left Stuart.

Is Stress a State of Mind?

Although the gripes of first-year law students (often called "one-Ls") and freshmen seemed similar, I was unaware of the amount of work that law school entails. One of my informants, Michelle, revealed that she

spent her first year reading about eight hundred pages a week. She emphasized the "huge" difference between college and law school academics: "I
would literally get up and do nothing but read, go to classes, and then go
to bed. My life *drastically* changed when I entered law school. . . . I was *used*
to being competitive, and [even though] BC has a reputation . . . for being
pretty laid back . . . I was *shocked* at the competitiveness between the students for grades and to do well." Although Michelle felt that "certainly the
first year's the worst year," she admitted that stress is a matter of choice:
"There are two different issues: do you have the time, and should you make
the time." She confirmed that although the "workload stays the same, you
become more efficient."

According to one-L Nicole (a pseudonym), "The workload is somewhat manageable; it's being surrounded by the smartest people from schools
all around the country" that yields the stress." (Prior to my research, I was
not aware that "our" law school is ranked number twenty-two in the nation.) Another one-L, Missy, came up and corroborated the stress of law
school, which she is experiencing firsthand. I was pleased with her eager-
ness to give me her perspective, even though she mostly seemed to want a
diversion from working on a paper. For her, researching and studying on a
Saturday is a common, unfortunate occurrence. She admitted that she and
many of her peers often spend weekends working. On Saturdays and Sundays Missy routinely wakes up at 9:00 A.M., runs, and then retreats to what
she calls the Stuart "snack bar." According to Missy, only the "wacky people"
go to the library, because they "can't handle the pressure." She prefers the
casual and quiet atmosphere of "Stu's." She even commented that "if you're
a wack job in college, you'll be a head case in law school." Missy then explained that although the stress is bad, "you can make it worse for yourself."
She also broke down the process of law school: the first year is very stressful, the second year is a little less so because the students can choose their
classes, and the stress returns the third year as everyone competes for jobs.
She joked about how "pathetic" her life is, yet reassured me that she tries
not to let law school consume her. She insisted that "you can't let [the first
year] spoil the rest of your experience." Missy wrapped up our conversation by offering some advice for aspiring lawyers: "If you can laugh at law
school, you're in good shape." (If good humor doesn't do the trick, a legal
magazine recommends a "law dictionary discus throw" to make law school
more fun [Stabile 43].)

A couple of weeks later, I spoke with John, Sue, and Chris (all third-
year students), a mellower group who seemed to have the whole law school
thing under control. Contradicting Missy, John claimed that the program is

"not as intensive as everyone thinks." He even admitted to working harder
as an undergraduate. Sue commented that it's just a matter of adjustment.
Chris contributed little, opting to keep his head buried in a textbook. However, all three agreed that there is *definitely* time to participate in outside
interests. In fact, when I approached their group, they weren't even discussing legal matters; John was reading *USA Today* and Sue was filling in a
crossword puzzle. However, they did warn me that perhaps they were the
wrong people to ask; for whatever reasons, they had not done much work
their first year.

Socrates Who?

Having heard so much about the workload, I wondered how different law school lectures are from undergraduate courses. According to
my informants, law professors emphasize the Socratic method, in which
discussion is given full rein and there little or no direct instruction. Lin-
guist/ethnographer Susan Urmston Philips finds the method has remained
relatively consistent over the years. First, the teacher calls on a student by
courtesy title (Mr. or Ms.) and last name, whether or not he or she has vol-
unteered to speak. This student is then asked a series of questions, each
one being "structurally and topically dependent" on his or her last response
(1–2). Missy commented that although this method is not used all the time,
most professors encourage their students to think for themselves and try to
teach them to be problem solvers.

However, most of my other informants viewed this method in a
more negative light. One study of female one-Ls attributes the stressful
environment of law school to the Socratic method: "Females speak less in
class for fear of being ridiculed or devalued by their professors and in turn
devalue their own ability" (Ellsworth 1474). Nicole claimed, "You just care
what your classmates think about you; you want to sound like you know
what you're talking about. . . . So unfortunately a lot of people stress out in
class cause they don't know if they're going to be called on. . . . They've
read the material, but they don't know if they've digested the material."

Male students also experience classroom anxiety. Edward Shlikas,
a former student at Wake Forest University Law School, was so disgusted
by the Socratic method that he has filed a $125 million lawsuit and staged
a hunger strike ("Wake" 11). In his effort to eliminate the use of the Socratic
method, Shlikas hopes to bring about better treatment of students. He
blames professors for piling "tons of work" on students in order to "break
[them] down" and "weed [them] out." Insisting that he and his counter-

parts were treated as "subhumans," Shlikas also attributes weight loss, depression, headaches, and fatigue to the pressures brought to bear by professors. According to Shlikas, certain professors even threaten to humiliate students who are not adequately prepared for class. Although he realizes that losing this case could ruin his chances of becoming a lawyer, he feels he has a moral obligation to move forward with the lawsuit. Although a date for the preliminary hearing has not yet been set, he hopes his efforts will be acknowledged and possibly rewarded.

Michelle offered her perspective as both a teacher and a law student. She currently teaches an undergraduate environmental law course along with one of her peers, Julie. As a teacher, she views the Socratic method as an "autodidactic" approach in which she and Julie do not "do most of the talking" but instead allow their students to voice their opinions and express their knowledge. Although as a student she admits feeling "weird" lecturing rather than being lectured to, she sees the implementation of this method as a necessary teaching tool.

Administration Accessibility: Woeful or Wondrous

One day I spoke with three male students who were "supposed to be studying." An African named De expounded on the educational process while one of his companions, Steve, chomped messily on his chicken-salad-on-pumpernickel. De complained that he had yet to learn the law after three years and consequently had to shell out an extra thousand dollars to take a prep course for the bar. He admitted, however, that it was neither BC's nor the professors' fault that the law students had to "teach themselves." The professors, he affirmed, are actually "great people" who are very accessible, even though his contact with them is often limited to either a game of "hoops" or a night of social drinking.

When I asked the group of mellow third-year students about the controversy surrounding the impending replacement of Dean Avram Soifer, a liberal Jew, both John and Sue claimed that they had not been given any information. They asserted that in general the students do not know what is going on. John felt the administration could be more responsive to student needs and connected the controversial Soifer situation to the influence of Father Leahy, the current president of Boston College. Supposedly Leahy views Soifer as a potential threat to the integrity of Boston College's reputation as a Jesuit institution. Although Sue admitted that the Catholic influence is less prevalent in the law school than in the undergraduate college, where one is likely to find "crosses in the window," both she and John were not enthused about the possible increase in Jesuit control.

Missy also claimed that the administration could be a little more helpful and said she did not want Father Leahy to get greater control of the law school. Nicole, on the other hand, asserted that the administration is "absolutely great. They're so supportive and so good." However, she did admit to seeing "little" problems on campus, which she attributed not necessarily to the administration but to the students.

Is Minority Enrollment an Issue?

It was not until the second half of the twentieth century that women, minorities, and members of the lower classes were admitted into esteemed institutions, including law schools (Granfield 333). Although the legal profession has made great strides, a number of BCLS students expressed racial and gender concerns.

As an African American female, Nicole sees many loopholes both within BCLS and in the legal system itself. She suggested that perhaps the issue of race is somewhat suppressed. She pointed out, "BC is not a diverse institution at all. . . . I think the numbers are saaaaad in my section." Out of the hundred and five people in her section, only five are African American, a situation which she called "ludicrous." She also noted that her community-law professor, who is white, once claimed this number as evidence of how far blacks have come as a society. In retaliation, Nicole attempted to respond that this was, in fact, "*no* progress at all. . . . I just kept raising my hand but he would not pick on me. . . . I'm assuming he graduated from law school maybe twenty-five years ago. . . . I was astounded." This professor had also trumpeted the current fifty-fifty male-to-female ratio, but he had failed to mention that only four women in that 50 percent are black. In reference to her peers, Nicole claimed, "Generally speaking, I mean in terms of race relations, I guess things are fine. . . . It's sort of hard to say though. People don't talk about race a lot in class, and, again, I think that people are afraid of saying, what they feel, and I wish that people would . . . I love the comments that are ignorant because they challenge me." She also said: "I feel that it's a competitive atmosphere, definitely, and I feel that some of the people in the class don't see the people of color as competition. And I think that's really disturbing, and I just think they underestimate the hard work that we've put into getting where we are today."

Although Nicole may dispute the phrase, the last thirty years have seen an "opening up" of law schools to women and people of color. Law schools "have been using race and ethnicity as positive factors in order to achieve a diverse student body" rather than relying on LSAT scores or undergraduate grade-point averages. The admissions process is more than just a numbers game: "It is about real people with real dreams . . . about taking risks and admitting people who are different [and] whose backgrounds suggest they will make different but important contributions. . . . If we could persuade the public that law schools and the profession are looking for lawyers with a sense of justice, compassion, and commitment to service . . . even though their test scores are not that high, we might find that the public perception of lawyers might improve" (Romero 55).

Despite these efforts, recent attacks on equal-opportunity admissions practices have given way to a rapid decline in affirmative-action policies. Rates of enrollment among students of color have dropped tremendously, as reported at UC Berkeley's law school. "These trends portend a return to the law school of the 1960s" and have hampered efforts at "transforming the face of the legal profession" (Romero 54). When I asked Nicole her opinion on the affirmative-action movement, she asserted: "I'm clearly pro–affirmative action. I think that a lot of the issues surrounding affirmative action have to do with society—they don't understand what it means. As far as they're concerned, it means that black people have privileges, and that white people don't have them. That is *not* what it's about. . . . I'm clearly here because of affirmative action, but it doesn't mean that I didn't work as hard as the white person that's sitting right next to me. . . . It doesn't mean that my LSAT scores are lower, it doesn't mean that my application was not as good, if not *better.*" Apparently, what Nicole initially identified as "little" issues are in fact serious matters that she feels need to be addressed and, if possible, remedied.

Although it is apparent that Nicole has a few bones to pick with the law school, several of my other informants did not see diversity as a real obstacle. Most seemed relatively satisfied with ethnic representation. One informant said she finds BCLS "less stuffy" compared with other law schools. According to her, students here are very willing to help one another out, so much so that it's almost "family-like." Since she and most of her peers are financing their own education and share the same focus, which is training for a career, she feels there are actually fewer economic differences between BCLS students than between Boston College undergraduates.

Defending the Defenders

Having acquired some knowledge of the academic climate, I wanted to find out the "real" information—why, exactly, are these people in law school? what kinds of law do they hope to practice? Missy put it very well:

it depends on the type of person one is. Then too, many law students don't know what kind of law they want to practice, or if they want to practice at all. Missy commented that it is very common these days for people to attend law school just to become well rounded.

Missy herself is specifically interested in child law, with a side interest in property and the environment. Her focus is families: aiding abused kids and dealing with custody, guardianship, and divorce. Like many of her peers, her involvement goes beyond the classroom. She volunteers at night in the emergency room of the Boston Medical Center, counseling victims of domestic violence. She provides legal help for these women and places them in shelters, if necessary. Missy said that while working with these women is personally fulfilling it has also sharpened her interviewing and client-advocacy skills. She hopes that through courtroom litigation she can help women in need. Although she has observed that many older lawyers become burned out emotionally over the years, Missy sees a greater purpose behind her personal involvement: "The more I know them, the more I'll fight for them."

Nicole also professed an interest in abused women, particularly those of color. "I am basically here because I think there is a lot of inherent racism in our judicial system . . . and I am trying to find a way to, I hate to use this phrase, but to free people of color, essentially, and free people who are poor . . . to become the voice of the voiceless." She is going to work in Cambridge this summer at Somerville Legal Services, a "really well known" New England firm. Through her upcoming work as part of a team representing battered women involved in custody battles, Nicole hopes to "serve the poor community and again, those women of color who can't get out of abusive relationships. . . . Whatever I decide to do, nonprofit [service] is going to be part of it."

Michelle, the environmental law teacher, also proved to be extremely dedicated. I was pleasantly surprised to find out that she was teaching this undergraduate course out of choice, not obligation. Although she is quite sure that teaching will not be her profession, she did express a great enthusiasm for pedagogy. Although Michelle has always felt strongly about protecting the environment, wildlife, and animals, law school was not always in the picture. In fact, she spent four years "fumbling, trying to figure out what [she] wanted to do." She considered veterinary school for quite some time, and worked as a veterinary assistant; but she became so frustrated with the mistreatment of pets by owners that she abandoned that field. It was not until her yearlong stay in England that she began to appreciate the stability of the U.S. legal system and the "highly developed country we live in." This change in viewpoint, that laws can be used "as tools to protect the environment," subsequently led Michelle to law school.

According to Sue and John, the self-professed first-year "slackers," few people come to law school knowing what kind of law they want to practice. Perhaps Nicole, Missy, and Michelle are exceptions. John expressed an interest in the law in general pretty early on, since late high school, while Sue did not consider a legal profession in litigation until college. John commented that a law school education is quite expensive and that he has to work a part-time job to help pay for it. John also told me that the mean age of law students is twenty-seven; most students take time off after college before they decide to go back to school.

Money, Money, Money

The three friendly men I encountered in Stuart one Saturday morning, Lawrence, Steve, and De, seemed very concerned about financial prosperity. Lawrence expressed an interest in the infamous realm of corporate law; De wanted to go into international litigation; Steve's target was house council or international business. Although they always knew they wanted to be lawyers, they had some legitimate advice: don't go into law unless you're absolutely sure you want to, and study or travel abroad first if possible. They mentioned that some people do not practice after law school and that a few don't even take the bar, which is fine with them: it cuts the competition for jobs. Steve claimed there is a "big pay difference" between large and small firms and suggested that location is a prime factor in the prosperity of a business. The three joked with me quite a bit and were rather defensive at times, cautioning, "Don't take this down." Although their motives may not be purely monetary, they seemed to emphasize the importance of prestige and size in employment prospects. At the same time, they were quick to defend the legal profession.

Is There Such a Thing as a "Good" Lawyer?

Although some of my informants dismissed the negative image of lawyers, many understood the reason for it. Missy said she had never wanted to work in a large firm and had never considered corporate law. She, too, associates corporate law with money; however, she also said that women are equally represented in the various fields. She pointed out that many people have a misconception that males dominate corporate law, while the more "sensitive" females are more likely to join advocacy-based legal arenas. She supported her argument by saying, "Many guys are interested in kids and domestic violence too." Her statement helped me realize that perhaps De, Steve, and Lawrence are not representative of all male law students.

When I asked whether lawyer jokes are valid, most of the law students said there is little justification for them. De and Steve claimed that only a very few lawyers fit the generalizations made by the public. De felt it was a case of "blaming the messenger." He argued that the lawyer is often wrongfully blamed for the problems inherent to a society. According to De, even those who make the jokes will need the services of a lawyer at one point or another. Another misconception, which Steve addressed, is that all lawyers are wealthy. He warned, "Don't be fooled by the numbers that BC puts out." Nicole could understand why lawyers have a bad reputation, but at the same time she thinks there are "a lot of positive lawyers out there who really believe in justice and have principles about equality and about what's right and wrong." She added, "If people really believed the stereotypes, I don't know what would happen." Likewise, John accepted the fact that people poke fun at lawyers (he brought up the"slip-and-fall" television commercials as one of the reasons) but thinks it is important for people to recognize the important function that lawyers have in society. John also mentioned that at a good law school, it's hard to "pick out who's going to be the big lawyers."

Michelle came out with the biggest shocker. Prior to law school, she thought lawyers were "slimy, greedy, and interested in money." In fact, when her college professors suggested she apply to law school, she took it as an insult. She was also blunt in her opinion of her peers. She finds most of them "uptight" and usually doesn't socialize with them: "They're not down to earth about things. Most . . . are pretty interested in how much money they can make, what their grades are, and what prestigious job they're being offered, and frankly, that makes me nauseous."

Yes, Law Students Do Have Lives

All of my informants emphasized the importance of time management. Many of the older law students simply don't have the time to stay on campus after class. They have other commitments, such as holding jobs and raising families.

I was impressed with Michelle's creative streak. She is interested in ceramics (she had glazed and fired a vase for a friend who had been a guest speaker for one of her lectures), dabbles in furniture making, and used to play professional tennis. Michelle's teaching partner, Julie, prefers aerobics and dance as her outlet, and visits her long-term boyfriend in New Jersey on the weekends. (She admitted that making time for her relationship requires a great deal of effort and energy.)

Speaking of significant others, for many of the law students, marriage is not a distant prospect, nor is it uncommon for them to have friends who are either married or engaged. However, John asserted that although some "BCLSers" have families, he tends to socialize with people closer to his age, in their mid to late twenties.

Lawyers Are People Too

Although I was hesitant to initiate conversation with the law students, once I did I was able to relinquish my fear. Much to my surprise, I realized they are real people with real concerns and are not in fact invincible. For example, following our lengthy interview, Michelle discovered she had locked her keys in her car; I was reassured to find her so unmistakably *human*. Moreover, most of my informants did not view themselves as being superior. Although some responses reaffirmed my perception of lawyers as uptight and money-hungry, there were far more exceptions to the rule. Perhaps these displays of humanitarianism, humor, and frustration are not a mere coincidence. I now respect the BCLS students not as ambitious "elders," but as strong people with goals, lives, and the occasional hurdle to overcome. I can now sit in Stuart with ease . . . if only those law students would keep their voices down. Did I forget to mention how noisy they can get during lunch?

Works Cited

Chiseri-Strater, Elizabeth, and Bonnie Stone Sunstein. *Fieldworking: Reading Writing Research.* Prentice Hall, 1997.

Ellsworth, Phoebe C. "Stress and Health in First-Year Students: Women Fare Worse." *Journal of Applied Social Psychology* 24 (1994): 1474–79.

Granfield, Robert. "Making It by Faking It: Working Class Students in an Elite Environment." *Journal of Contemporary Ethnography* 20 (1991): 331–51.

Philips, Susan Urmston. "The Language Socialization of Lawyers: Acquiring the Cant." In *Doing the Ethnography of Schooling,* edited by George Spindler, 176–209. New York: Holt, Rinehart, and Winston, 1982..

Romero, Leo. "Law Schools: Measures of Merit and the Public's Perception of the Legal Profession." *Black Issues in Higher Education* 14 (1997): 54–55.

Rosenbaum, Wayne S. "The Law Offices of Wayne S. Rosenbaum: Lawyer Jokes." On-line. Available: enlaw@lawinfo.com

Stabile, Tom. "10 Ways to Make Law School More Fun." *The National Jurist,* March/April 1998, 43–44.

"Wake Forest University: Law Student on Strike Over Socratic Method." *The National Jurist,* March/April 1998, 11.

Quiet Please

Laura Sarrasin

❦

For two weekends every summer my sister woke up early to watch Wimbledon on television. This is one of the four major tennis tournaments held each year. Wimbledon is played in England, at the All England Lawn and Croquet Club, and is considered the most prestigious tournament of all. When I came downstairs on those hot weekend mornings, my sister would be sprawled out on the couch with everything she could possibly need for the day. It was clear that she would be monopolizing the television and that I would have to find somewhere else to watch the Red Sox game. Half awake, I would plop down in the recliner with my cereal and OJ and watch a few points. When I was done with my breakfast, I'd rise from the chair with a sigh and set out to find another television.

On one of those mornings, I realized the match was played in silence. It was so quiet in the stadium that you could hear a pin drop on the grass court! When I asked my sister why this was, she replied (her eyes still glued to the television) that tennis was a game of skill and the players needed silence in order to concentrate. Being a big baseball fan and an obnoxious eight-year-old, I said that baseball players needed to concentrate too, but they played with screaming crowds in the background. She told me tennis was a much more civilized sport and to shut up.

I never gave this matter another thought until this past summer, when I was riding in the car with my father on a hot summer afternoon. He asked me if I had heard about the new Arthur Ashe Stadium. I had taken up tennis the summer before I entered high school and had since found myself getting up early on weekend mornings to watch Wimbledon instead of the Red Sox game. Since tennis had become a part of my life, I knew the facts behind the stadium, but I didn't know about the controversy.

The Arthur Ashe Stadium is a new tennis facility in Queens, New York. It was named after tennis great Arthur Ashe, an African American who died of AIDS a few years ago. The new stadium is part of an expansion project on Flushing Meadows in Flushing, New York, the site of the annual U. S. Open. This is another one of the four major tournaments and begins about two months after Wimbledon, in late August. Flushing Meadows is right next to one of New York City's major airports, La Guardia. Planes coming into and going out of New York City fly over the stadium all the time. Sometimes, because of the tremendous noise that the airplanes produce, play is stopped. Players in the U. S. Open have had to try to block out the noise and play through it. The Arthur Ashe Stadium will have the same problem. The United States Tennis Association (USTA) entered into an agreement with the City of New York under former mayor David Dinkins that no planes are allowed to fly over the stadium while a match is being played. If any airplane violates this agreement, they are fined a large sum of money ("Giuliani").

The Arthur Ashe Stadium opened September 23, 1997, two days before the U. S. Open was scheduled to begin. There was a grand-opening celebration featuring many past and present tennis greats. Naturally, the mayor of New York City, Rudolf Giuliani, was invited to the celebration. The mayor declined his invitation. He sees the agreement between the USTA and the airport as foolish. In his opinion, it is ridiculous that hundreds of planes have to be rerouted so that a tennis match can be played in silence. The mayor fully intends to boycott all events at the stadium ("Giuliani").

When my father finished telling me all the details, he said he agreed with Mayor Giuliani. As I did in the family room ten years ago, he brought up baseball players and screaming crowds. Why can baseball players play in clamorous atmospheres while tennis players need silence? Is it because tennis needs more concentration than a sport like baseball? But is this really true? Is it that much harder to concentrate on a tennis match than on a baseball game? Players and coaches of both sports have very different views on this matter. Carl LaBranche, head coach of men and women's tennis at Providence College, says, "It does not take more concentration than baseball or anything else for that matter." I wondered if somewhere, buried in the history of tennis, there was a reason that matches were kept silent.

In 1873 Englishman Major Walter Clopton Wingfield patented lawn tennis. Since the sport had been around since the early days of history, Wingfield was simply "the obstetrician who brought forth the infant" (Potter, 8). Lawn tennis would later thrive as a competitive sport at The All England Croquet Club. The club was founded in 1868 and was strictly a croquet club for its first few years. Croquet was fast becoming a dead sport when Wingfield patented tennis. The people who ran the All England thought that if they converted some of their lawns into tennis courts, they would bring in more revenue. Soon the club changed its name to the All England Lawn and Croquet Club. Lawn tennis became the sole source of the club's profits. Since this new sport was being played at a private club, it drew very wealthy players and spectators (Potter, 9–11). LaBranche says, "Tennis in its original form was considered a gentleman's game; therefore silence as a spectator was the proper behavior. It has stayed with this tradition for absolutely no reason." This makes the atmosphere of a tennis match very unique. It has always been very different from the mood of a barbaric sport like baseball.

Baseball is America's favorite pastime. It is inherent to our culture. "Ever since our cavemen ancestry, men and boys liked to hit something that resembled a ball with a club" (Lieb, 3). Alexander J. Cartwright is said to be the father of modern American baseball. He organized the first baseball club, the Knickerbocker Base Ball Club of New York, in 1845 (Lieb, 18). Other clubs soon formed and joined to create a league. Baseball was primarily a game played and watched by the "working class." On their way home from work men would sometimes gather around a field where a game was being played. They would cheer the players on and show their excitement throughout the game. Baseball became a source of entertainment (Lieb, 15).

In some stadiums, as many as eighty thousand people are able to watch a baseball game. Fans carry on their private conversations, talking and laughing. Cries of "Peanuts here!" and "Hot dogs, get your hot dogs!" are heard constantly all over the ballpark. The crowd goes wild when a ball is hit deep, even if the left fielder is trying to catch it. No one tells the fans to quiet down during play. Sometimes the people who run the scoreboard encourage the fans to make noise. Baseball players are used to noise. They are able to block it all out. This is something that most tennis players have a great deal of difficulty doing.

At a tennis match, times when one can cheer or even move are very limited. When you sit down to watch a tennis match, chances are you'll be stuck there for the next three hours or so. Unless you are close to an exit, getting out of the stands can be difficult, for fans are usually not allowed to leave during play. Some players have complained that seeing fans move around in the stands draws their attention away from the ball. After a point is scored, the crowd always cheers and shouts out words of encouragement to the player of their choice. As the players walk back to the service lines, the chair umpire reaches for his microphone and politely asks the fans to quiet down. There have been instances where security has escorted unruly fans out of a match. Noise proves to be a great distraction for most tennis players.

In most sporting events, noise is a given. Athletes must have the ability to block things out and adjust to changes in the sound around them. How well players adapt to the noise usually influences their success (Moran, 110–11). Players having a good day are able to block everything out. They are in the "zone"; they cannot miss. On the other hand, if players are making one error after another, every little sound is likely to bother them. Specifically in tennis, hearing outside noise may keep a player from hearing the sound of their opponent's racket. Expert tennis players can predict the shot coming at them by listening to the way the ball hits the strings of their opponent's racket. Outside noise lessens their ability to "read" the shot and pushes them out of the "zone." In a 1992 Wimbledon match, Nathalie Tauziat of France complained that Monica Seles was grunting as she hit the ball and thus preventing Tauziat from hearing the sound that the ball made against Seles's racket (Moran, 111).

When players are confronted with a sudden change in the level of noise, as Tauziat was, they are immediately distracted. A tennis player is used to complete silence. A sudden noise like a sneeze, or even a less sudden noise like an airplane flying overhead, distracts them greatly. Baseball players are used to the hum of the crowd. If they are faced with silence, their nerves are all aflutter, and it is very hard to concentrate. When athletes get used to certain situations, it is very hard for them to adapt to new conditions. I too was one of these athletes that found it very hard to concentrate in certain situations.

I was playing in my championship softball game. It was the bottom of the ninth inning. The bases were loaded, there were two outs, and I was up to bat. I stepped out of the dugout and onto the chocolate-colored dirt. The crowd was buzzing. I walked toward home plate and glanced around the field, seeing hundreds of eyes, all staring at me. The pitcher stood tall on the circular "mound." Her confident eyes met my terrified ones as I approached the plate. I stepped into the batter's box, the familiar hum of the crowd calming me. I dug my feet into the dirt and then took a few practice swings. The pitcher brought her arm up into her glove and looked at the catcher for the sign. Suddenly, a hush fell over the crowd. It was so quiet I could hear people squirming nervously in their seats. A million thoughts ran through my mind. I was beginning to lose focus on the game. Suddenly, the ball whizzed by me; I hadn't even known the pitcher had thrown it. How was I ever going to concentrate without the familiar hum of the crowd?

But I found myself distracted by little noises in the crowd while playing tennis later that year. It was a warm day in early fall, and I was playing in a high school tennis match. The score was tied; each team had won three matches. The outcome of my match would be the deciding point. The other members of both teams had gathered on the grass beyond the fence that enclosed court 3. Thirty pairs of eyes watched my every move. With much effort, I had finally worked my way up to match point. My opponent hit me the ball that she had just slammed into the net and I caught it with my racket. As I turned around to walk back to the service line, I saw all the spectators sprawled out on the grass, watching. My teammates shouted words of encouragement as I readied myself to serve. When I approached the service line, I looked up and saw my opponent jumping up and down at the other end of the court. I brought my arm up to my forehead and wiped the sweat from my face. I bounced the fluorescent yellow ball a few times and spun my racket in my clammy hand. I took a deep breath and tossed the ball into the bright blue sky. I bent my knees and thrust my racket into the air to meet the ball. Suddenly I heard a sneeze somewhere behind me. I finished my swing just in time to see the ball slam right into the bottom of the net. I reached into my pocket for another ball and hoped for the silence that I was used to.

Sitting in the family room on that warm summer morning I'd hit upon something that can't really be explained. There is no concrete reason why tennis is played in silence. The sport has always been played this way and will probably continue to abide by this tradition for many years to come. Throughout all my years of playing tennis, I never really thought that tennis took any more concentration than a sport like baseball. I just thought that it was a great sport, with a very special tradition.

Works Cited

"Giuliani Boycotts U. S. Open Over `No-Fly' Rule." *The New York Times.*
   August 26, 1997.

LaBranche, Carl (Head Coach of Men and Women's Tennis, Providence
   College, Providence, Rhode Island). Telephone Interview, October 21,
   1997.

Lieb, Frederick. *The Baseball Story.* New York: G. P. Putnam's Sons, 1950.

Moran, Aidan. *The Psychology of Concentration in Sports Performances: A
   Cognitive Analysis.* London: Psychology Press, 1996.

Potter, E. C. *Kings of the Court.* New York: Charles Scribner's Sons, 1936.

Part Six

Satire and Irony

It's All About the Uniform

Simon O'Connell

❦

I'm not a fashion "goo-roo." I've never been hip to the latest trends. I never owned a hypercolor T-shirt or a pair of those Andre Agassi–inspired spandex-denim shorts. I never saw the point of Reebok pumps. I take that back. My mother never allowed me to see the point of Reebok pumps. These fads went as quickly as they came.

Uniforms, on the other hand, transcend all temporal boundaries. Boston College is a private university, and it just wouldn't be right to go to a Catholic institution without a uniform to wear. Though less traditional than the white shirts and gray slacks of our younger days, there is an unofficial uniform worn by many male BC students. Maybe it's a need to conform; maybe it's about style. Regardless of the underlying reason, guys at BC have found a uniform to serve the purpose.

Let's start with those room keys dangling on a lacrosse string. They hang precariously out of the pocket, just waiting to get caught on a bush in front of Carney or snagged on an innocent fellow student's backpack. "You're just asking to lose your keys wearing them like that," I mutter to myself every time I pass one of these clones walking through the quad. (I can spot them from across the Dust Bowl, and after reading this, you'll be able to as well.) There is absolutely no way someone can argue that it is more practical to dangle keys out of the pocket rather than tuck them safely away where they belong. Unfortunately, when they're not hanging keys down their leg, club members are swinging the damn things on their fingers. Not only is this incredibly annoying to someone trying to carry on a conversation with the swinger, but he or she is liable to get an eye knocked out.

Next, those keys can't be hanging out of any old pocket. Khakis are the pants of choice! Make sure they're wrinkle free though, because these pants are going to be well worn. Newcomers to the club, be advised:

three to four pairs are needed, because these threads are versatile! Sweaters, T-shirts, and especially flannels all go well with these multipurpose pants. Not to be confused with the grunge look of the early nineties that took the nation's youth by storm, this uniform has the dressed-up-while-still-being-casual look going for it. . .so tuck those flannel shirttails in! Of course, some leniency is permitted. Undershirts are allowed as long as the plaid is buttoned down, top to bottom.

Personally, unless I'm wearing a tie, I never put my shirt in my pants. My father tucks his shirt in, and there is absolutely no way I am going to emulate the man that brought me into the world in a fashion statement that has long since passed him by. Still it's becoming increasingly obvious that others don't feel the same way. Now why is this the case, I ask? *Practicality?* To stay warm on those chilly New England evenings? Possibly. What about *comfort?* An unacceptable response, because true comfort is found in old jeans and sweatpants. Ah, it *looks* neat. Finally an inroad into the club. Style is what makes this uniform so popular. The look and image appeals to people.

So you're beginning to think you look pretty sharp? There is one final ingredient that separates members of the club from the rest of the student body. The white baseball cap has been designated the hat of choice. Just bought that hat and nervous you're going to stand out? Not to worry, new hats can be made to look old! After much probing and investigating, I discovered that the brim is given the tattered, quote-unquote well-used look by being quote-unquote keyed out. This art requires the uniform wearer to abrade the front of his cap with his keys until the covering fabric begins to peel away. Spend roughly five minutes doing this and you'll look like a veteran in no time. (An overly chaffed cap can be reinforced with staples.)

But hold on! There's more work to be done. Ever wonder why there's a button on top? Take it off! Remove it with a sharp object, if it doesn't give way to brute force first. You haven't had it on your head, but that hat is beginning to look like it's been around since the last time the Sox won the Series. However, it still needs some discoloration to become official. Wipe a little dirt on that puppy. Or better yet, get it grubby and wear it in the shower! This will add that sweat-ring look that all uniform wearers go for. One has to admit this is a hell of a lot of work, a seemingly pointless exertion of effort and time. But hey, this is about image, not time. Some even go so far as to say a hat is more than something worn, it's a part of you. The true uniform wearer knows whereof he speaks: you'll be lucky ever to see it off his head.

A few accessories can now be added. Ankle socks are the first. It's cold out, why the hell are people choosing to wear socks that barely cover the feet? Then again, I don't understand this uniform business to begin with. Another useless but widely worn accessory . . . the fleece vest. If you're really looking for a little warmth why not add sleeves to that Polartec so it can work it's magic? The vest is nothing more than a wind tunnel as far as I'm concerned. Last but not least, throw a little Phish into the CD player and you'll be all set.

Khakis show stains. White hats take an incredible amount of preparation only to end up looking messy. Hanging keys from lacrosse strings against the lower thigh is intensely impractical. Let's face it, this getup is all about style, so step out of your dorm room with confidence. Hey, let's be honest, you're looking good. Who said uniforms curb individuality?

What Time is it in Cyberspace?

Matt Koch

Trust me, totally stuck in the black hole of phones and letters was not how I wanted to spend my life. My parents, Mama Pterodactyl and Daddy Brontosaurus, thought that computers were electronic T-Rexes, and they sheltered me from this wave of the future. If these relics thought they were still in the Mesozoic era, how could they know anything about surfing the web? My outmoded parents totally devastated my life! In high school, all my friends communicated on-line with e-mail. Even off-line at Taco Bell, they would eat their seven-layer burritos while talking and laughing about their cool little e-mails. Meanwhile, all I could say was, "Could you guys give me some fire sauce for my burrito?" I was suuuch an outcast! I would try to get in touch with them by phone, but all I could do was leave messages on their answering machines that they never checked. Duh, it's the nineties, and nowadays people communicate with e-mail. I was like: help, save me from the ice age!

Finally, college came to the rescue, and I got hooked up with a computer, Ethernet card, e-mail account, and the appropriate software. My computer was so easy to use that within five minutes I was rockin' 'n' rollin', e-mailing my friends in Chicago, Boston, LA, Colorado, and Minnesota. I had become a computer nerd, but my popularity ironically skyrocketed. In a week, I was receiving ten-plus e-mails a day and feeling like a member of the generation.

Like the toppings on a nacho supreme, e-mail equals entropy. Say random things, and it's totally entertaining. The e-mail gig totally fit my personality; I could be lazy and not check grammar or spelling. Abbreviations like LOL (laughing out loud), BRB (be right back) and WTF (what the !@#$&?) really made communicating easy. I even got into the chain-letter thing, sending one message to all my friends simultaneously! Oh yeah, I received things too. I got funky letters with skeletons and spaceships made of periods, commas, hyphens, and semicolons. And most important, if my friends were like, way bummed, I would forward them funky stories and poems to cheer them up. The ice caps had melted.

But a few months ago, I received this e-mail:

Date: Tue. 16 Nov 1997 10:39:50
From: Tacoboy<j- Reedl@nwu.edu>
To: Matt<dailyp@bc.edu>
Subject: e-mail sux

Matt, I don't know when you are going to get this; I just got an e-mail from you today (11-16) that was from September 12. A two-month lag in e-mail could be a problem. I hope you even get this, because we need to figure what's wrong here. Oh, yeah since you asked, the food here is just ok. —Jeff

Wowwww! What had happened? I had sent hundreds of messages in the past, and they all went through smoothly, like free refills of Mountain Dew. So I just ignored Jeff's message and wrote him back and bragged that there was a Taco Bell near BU. The next day, he e-mailed and said that he had just received another message from me that was again two months overdue. I was frustrated and my head was screwy. How could the electronic age have let me down?

Oh no, I thought, I'm a victim of a cyber traffic jam. I had heard of cyber congestion before, delayed responses and messages traveling millions of extra cyber miles before getting through. Some cork in a lab was making second-rate microprocessors or something. The mere thought angered me, evil corporations dumping cheap technology on the market. Or maybe the problem was with Jeff's computer. Or one of his servers could have crashed. Or worse, maybe he was trying to hide his bingeing on soft-shell chicken tacos.

A bit later, I received this e-mail from my grandfather:

Date: Fri. 19 Nov 1997 19:45:43
From: Robert Daily <rDaily@iglou.com>
To: dailyp@bc.edu
Subject: Problem

Dear Matt,

Hesitate to inform you that your computer has the wrong date in it. Your letter is dated Friday, September 15, 1997.

Presume that somehow in moving the computer from where you got it to your room and reinstalling it that the date got messed up. Time appears to be off a little too. Your computer shows it was sent at 11:30 and we received it at 10:55 this morning.

MY computer has a button bar in the lower right corner that controls these things.

Thanks a lot for the neat letter !!!!!!!!!!

Grampa

So is this story totally embarrassing or what? And how about the awful truth that I sometimes communicate on-line with my archaic grampa? Anyway, I checked my computer and, yep, the clock was set two months early. It really makes me feel like a weenie, 'cuz the old man was right. Well, I gotta go. My bean burrito is getting cold.

Graffiti: Beyond This World

Troy Beaulieu, Daisy Cook, Greg Franzone, Marc Manganiello and Doug McMahon

❧

We have finally arrived on so-called planet Earth. Since this planet has never been explored in detail, we will attempt to decipher its inhabitants' social system by analyzing human writings on different structures throughout the former city of "Boston," mostly around an area known as "Chestnut Hill."

The first day: After debarking, we explored the surrounding area. Most buildings lay in ruins. We immediately realized that this species was somewhat different from what we had expected. Their society appears to have been crude and archaic, certainly much less refined than our own and ignorant of the intellectual pursuits we deeply value. From what we observed, we assume they had the odd practice of writing religious and monarchical inscriptions in various places. It also seems that integrated into this religious system was a heavy emphasis on sexuality. After further searching, we concluded that these engravings are located in three key areas, referred to in the vernacular as "bathrooms," "libraries," and "public property."

In the coming days, we will explore each area at length. We hope that what little remains of this world's civilization can be accurately reconstructed to produce a vignette of human life. We will report back when the fiery ball of Arcon (it seems humans referred to it as the "sun") rises over the plane again.

The second day: Recurring square, tiled "bathrooms," notable for their cleanliness and rows of partitioned thrones, are indicative of an aristocratic society with many rulers and royal families. Strangely, the bases of the thrones are bowl-like structures half-filled with water, as if water or liquid played some central role in religious ideology or government administration. Perhaps it merely had ceremonial significance. Individuals were not considered as equals here, proving that members of this society were certainly not an enlightened group. Clearly only a select few were worthy to sit on these thrones, for it is evident that the number provided could not possibly have matched the actual quantity needed for every human. Taller cleansing receptacles along the sides of the walls of the rooms indicate that the people had to wash their hands before meeting with their great rulers. Repeated references to this great being "god" have been found, most interestingly in the comment, "I've worshipped the porcelain god here." We are not sure exactly what to make of this, for in different buildings with similar such "bathrooms" this being is referred to as MC Hammer, Doug Flutie, Michael Jordan, and Hendrix. In one throne room we even found a statement claiming, "Mary rules!"

The third day: We have found a place identified as an "O'Neill Library." Not knowing what to make of this name, which is displayed on various other buildings in the northeast sector of this body of land, we consulted explorers from our neighboring planet Ishkibbible and discovered that O'Neill was a prominent figure in the culture. Inside another "library" they had found a book discussing something called the "Baseball Hall of Fame"; this book had further identified O'Neill as "Paul."

Within the "O'Neill Library" we found approximately twenty cubicles, each about five cubic picinkia in size. The walls of these cubicles contained inscriptions as well: "Calculus is pointless," "This library sucks," and "I want to get out of here" are examples of those we found. Perhaps these writings were prayers of desperation to the gods. These humans were clearly a disgruntled, easily angered, and fearful people. No doubt this negative attitude contributed to the violence and destruction that obliterated their planet.

It does appear that the humans' quest for knowledge, although incredibly misguided, was deeply rooted in the religious and spiritual realm. There was clearly much controversy over religion. The inscriptions are often scribbled out, marked over, or defaced. Because we found very few artifacts pertaining to O'Neill inside the building, it seems obvious that other religious groups came in and defaced the cubicles, or prayer sites. Perhaps there was a great religious debate that escalated into a sharp division among the population and soon brought them to the war and destruction that then destroyed every last human. The faithful people, perhaps in frustration at the violence and war, wrote their wishes to the gods, asking "Eat me" and pleading for "Nirvana." Were they crying out in vain to false gods for intervention?

The fact that these "library" buildings are meticulously arranged, with books in stacks and in neatly lined rows, only strengthens our belief that these were places of spiritualism. The gouges in the wood, stained with blue, black, and even green blood, are, it can be assumed, the remaining vestiges of religious sacrifices or ceremonies. This notion certainly parallels the evidence of barbarism uncovered during previous explorations. Whether the different-colored bloods came from multiple species we cannot positively conclude until we do scientific analysis back at Mother Bididong.

The final day: All our preconceived notions have been refuted. Was this some sort of hedonistic city that entwined religion with pleasure and indulgence? Were these abandoned buildings once whore houses, or were they sanctuaries in which priestesses performed sexual and religious acts? Painted on almost every visible surface are cryptic, perplexing phrases: "Sex is fun," "JR loves Joanna," and "Nick and Betty forever." What is the meaning of these seemingly endless messages?

If this society was all about "free love," why did the population deteriorate rather than expand? Perhaps they became disenchanted with their fellow humans, no longer finding each other sexually desirable, for on further exploration we encountered such messages as "I love dogs" and "Cats are the greatest." Maybe this decay was the result of a decline in religion, often the moral compass by which a society is directed. At any rate, these demented humans appear to have reverted to more primitive species. Their bestial tendencies may have come to dominate their rational capacities.

But perhaps there is a more plausible explanation for the lack of reproduction and the resulting extinction. We encountered strange glass cubicles placed intermittently throughout the city. Inside these cubicles are black boxes containing the inscription "Bell Atlantic" and a number panel into which codes were apparently punched. Writing scrawled on the glass walls uses such jargon as "For a good time call Julie." (This is repeated often, with other names substituted for Julie.) We surmise that these earthlings may have reproduced inside these glass cubicles while others watched and learned. Perhaps the cubicles were too scarce, as the "bathrooms" were. Maybe they didn't have adequate time to procreate.

Final analysis of planet Earth: Although we failed to encounter the "god" who took so many forms and so many different names (MC Hammer, Doug Flutie, etc.), this being appeared to be highly revered and respected as a leader. However, it seemed unable to control society, which appears to have regressed from a highly centralized, highly aristocratic state to one of pure chaos. Human beings seem to have allowed their society to deteriorate to the point of extinction.

There is a minority opinion among the members of our team regarding the etchings and markings we encountered throughout the planet. Some of us see these writings as mere gibberish and random expressions of random people's emotional state at the time. Possibly, these humans, acting impulsively and driven by pure emotion, simply wrote what they thought, felt, or wanted to express to others in random public places. Could all these writings signify absolutely nothing? We will probably never know.